Cambridge Elements

Elements in Politics and Communication
edited by
Stuart Soroka
University of California

AMPLIFYING EXTREMISM

Small Town Politicians, Media Storms, and American Journalism

Nik Usher
University of San Diego

Jessica C. Hagman
University of Illinois at Urbana-Champaign

Shaftesbury Road, Cambridge CB2 8EA, United Kingdom

One Liberty Plaza, 20th Floor, New York, NY 10006, USA

477 Williamstown Road, Port Melbourne, VIC 3207, Australia

314–321, 3rd Floor, Plot 3, Splendor Forum, Jasola District Centre, New Delhi – 110025, India

103 Penang Road, #05–06/07, Visioncrest Commercial, Singapore 238467

Cambridge University Press is part of Cambridge University Press & Assessment, a department of the University of Cambridge.

We share the University's mission to contribute to society through the pursuit of education, learning and research at the highest international levels of excellence.

www.cambridge.org
Information on this title: www.cambridge.org/9781009668781

DOI: 10.1017/9781009668798

© Nik Usher and Jessica C. Hagman 2025

This publication is in copyright. Subject to statutory exception and to the provisions of relevant collective licensing agreements, no reproduction of any part may take place without the written permission of Cambridge University Press & Assessment.

When citing this work, please include a reference to the DOI 10.1017/9781009668798

First published 2025

A catalogue record for this publication is available from the British Library

ISBN 978-1-009-66878-1 Hardback
ISBN 978-1-009-66875-0 Paperback
ISSN 2633-9897 (online)
ISSN 2633-9889 (print)

Additional resources for this publication at www.cambridge.org/Usher

Cambridge University Press & Assessment has no responsibility for the persistence or accuracy of URLs for external or third-party internet websites referred to in this publication and does not guarantee that any content on such websites is, or will remain, accurate or appropriate.

For EU product safety concerns, contact us at Calle de José Abascal, 56, 1°, 28003 Madrid, Spain, or email eugpsr@cambridge.org

Amplifying Extremism

Small Town Politicians, Media Storms, and American Journalism

Elements in Politics and Communication

DOI: 10.1017/9781009668798
First published online: May 2025

Nik Usher
University of San Diego

Jessica C. Hagman
University of Illinois at Urbana-Champaign

Author for correspondence: Nik Usher, nusher@sandiego.edu

Abstract: Within a week, a no-name Republican state representative from a town of 384 people in Illinois catapulted from obscurity to a prime-time appearance on Fox News' Ingraham Angle. This newly empowered politician, Darren Bailey, would go on to steer the pro-business Republican party in Illinois toward extremism. Democratic backsliding emerges across all levels of politics, but the threats posed by small town politicians have been overshadowed by national-level politicians. This microstudy of a single politician's debut in the public eye showcases a novel approach to media corpus construction that combines proprietary and open databases, aggregated search tools, and targeted searching, and includes local, regional, and national news across digital-first, radio, news publishers, broadcast and cable television, and social media. The Element provides unique insights into how American journalism creates space for small town extremists to gain power, especially given declines in local news.

Keywords: extremism, journalism, local news, partisan media, COVID

© Nik Usher and Jessica C. Hagman 2025

ISBNs: 9781009668781 (HB), 9781009668750 (PB), 9781009668798 (OC)
ISSNs: 2633-9897 (online), 2633-9889 (print)

Contents

Introduction — 1

1 Theorizing Extremist Politicians and the Democratic Press — 5

2 Methodology: The Case Study Corpus — 18

3 The Context and Structure for Illinois' Political and Media Ecosystems — 24

4 The Rise of Darren Bailey: PMP and the Political Economy of the News Industry — 33

5 Journalists, New Norms, and Amplifying Extremism — 52

6 Avoiding Accidental Amplification — 61

References — 72

Introduction

Over the course of a week, Darren Bailey, a first-term and little-known Republican state representative, catapulted from obscurity to a prime-time appearance on Fox News *Ingraham Angle*. His debut in front of a Fox audience averaging 3.6 million viewers a night (Katz, 2020) stemmed from his lawsuit challenging the Illinois governor's extension of a "safer-at-home" order in response to the COVID-19 pandemic. Certainly, the rapid rise of a small town politician from obscurity to a national figure is a well-trodden political narrative in US politics. What made Bailey's ascendency different is that he was not just a Republican challenging the Democratic governor; he was one of the first local politicians to garner prominence by resisting COVID-19 public health regulations.

His ascent has been described as a "highjacking" of the Illinois Republican party and a "big right turn" for a party previously known for its pro-business conservatism (Kapos, 2022). Bailey burst on the state political scene on April 23, 2020, when he filed his lawsuit challenging the extension of Governor J. B. Pritzker's "safer at home" emergency order and then earned further attention when his lawsuit resulted in a temporary restraining order exempting Bailey – and only Bailey – from the emergency order extension's provision (Corley, 2020). Within nine days of the lawsuit, right-wing protestors with Nazi signs began echoing Bailey's argument, contesting these stay-at-home powers in downtown Chicago and in the state capitol, Springfield.

In the two years that followed, Bailey would use his newfound fame to win a state Senate seat, announce his candidacy for the Republican gubernatorial primary, and win the Republican nomination for governor in 2022. After the 2020 presidential election, Bailey repeated Trump's unfounded claims of voter fraud on Twitter (now known as X) and signed a letter encouraging Republican US representative Mary Miller to vote against certifying the 2020 presidential election (Adams, 2021; Landis, 2021). Bailey lost the race for governor in 2022 but soon turned his eyes to the US House. He failed to secure Donald Trump's nomination and ultimately lost the primary to five-term Republican incumbent Mike Bost – whose positions were even further to the right than Bailey's (Kapos, 2023; Associated Press [AP], 2024).

Ironically, Bailey was a particularly ineffective legislator, sponsoring only one law that was ultimately passed (compared to three to sixteen bills passed by his Republican colleagues in the Illinois statehouse) (McKinney, 2022). And yet he was able to parlay his protest of COVID protection orders into brief political stardom. Bailey's political stances set him up as a standard-bearer of the Republican party's far-right politics in Illinois. Despite having limited actual political power, his political influence had far-reaching ramifications – possibly even emboldening antidemocratic activists with white nationalist proclivities.

Before his rise to fame, Bailey co-sponsored a bill forcing the expulsion of Chicago from Illinois and making it the fifty-first state (Bill Status of HR 0101, 2021), showing his willingness to draw on the discourse of downstate Illinois vs Chicago (McKinney, 2022). During his run for Congress with the support of the House Freedom Caucus (Cortes, 2024), Bailey continued to challenge state law; as a new assault weapon law went into effect, he posted a photo of himself on Twitter completing a puzzle surrounded by a collection of weapons and ammunition, challenging Pritzker to "knock on my door and take my guns" (Bailey, 2023). While Bailey was ultimately unsuccessful in his bid for power at the state and federal level, his case offers insight into the ways in which the ordinary work of journalism may serve to facilitate the rapid rise of extremist politicians, particularly in the context of social crisis. That he was out-primaried by an even more extremist politician in his race for Congress speaks to the polarization in the Republican party – and the antidemocratic and illiberal activists seeking to undermine the rule of law – from January 6, 2021, and beyond.

In this Element, we use Bailey's ascent as a case study and means of studying the link between micro actions by individual actors and the larger worlds of social structures (Ellis, 1999). The challenges from Bailey and others like him come at a time when local newspapers are cutting back on coverage and even closing; an estimated 1800 communities have lost access to daily, professional news about where they live (Abernathy, 2022). Indeed, local newspapers face an existential threat to their continued economic survival as trust in news media more generally has reached all-time lows. While scholarly and public attention often focuses on national media and national politics, state and local challenges often fly under the radar of elite stakeholders and public attention until those local unknowns push their way onto the national scene with extreme actions. By analyzing these cases, we can better understand the political and media conditions that facilitate the rise of extremist actors. We use this case study to examine two questions about American civic life and democratic culture:

1. What are the features of local political and media ecologies that might facilitate the rise of local politicians with extremist views?
2. How might journalism practices and norms, in combination with the structure of the contemporary news industry itself, serve to amplify these extremist actors?

We raise these questions in light of continued challenges to the rule of law across the US, where local politicians and officials have been emboldened to bring their politics to voting regulation, civic practices, and even disaster response with the potential for irreparable harm to individuals and the democratic project at large. Politics in the US have only grown more extreme since Bailey burst on the national and state consciousness during the initial days of COVID. The Republican party as a whole has moved right, with pro-business Conservativism being replaced with a more Trumpian brand of right-wing politics. Both backbenchers in the US Congress and small town politicians have been able to reliably generate media attention for their culture war antics. American journalism's long-standing vulnerabilities to extremist capture, the more contemporary market failure of journalism, and the runaway success of hyperpartisan digital media combined facilitate the rise of these politicians from obscurity to notoriety. Given these dynamics, Bailey's anti-COVID activism is a blueprint for how to win power and influence as an extremist politician in our contemporary media and political culture.

The Element consists of five main sections:

In Section 1, Theorizing Extremist Politicians and The Democratic Press, we begin with a brief timeline of Bailey's rise. We begin on April 23, 2020, when Bailey filed his lawsuit against Illinois Governor J. B. Pritzker, which argued that Pritzker abused his powers by extending Illinois' stay-at-home order. We end on May 2, 2020, when journalists reported on two events: Bailey's withdrawal of the lawsuit to make his case more broadly applicable and right-wing nationalist protests against the governor in Illinois featuring Nazi symbols and rhetoric. This period also covers his national media breakthrough: his appearance on Fox News' Ingraham Angle. We then turn to three disparate threads of political communication scholarship to ground our empirical inquiry: first, the Politics-Media-Politics (PMP) framework, second, the concept of "media storms," and third, a political economy approach to understanding the news media. A more extended timeline can be found in Online Appendix A.

In Section 2, Methodology: The Case Study Corpus, we offer the specific background for our case study and our approach to data gathering. We discuss the importance of conducting microanalysis and the main approaches to our data gathering: the creation of a media corpus across digital, local, partisan, state, and national news outlets and across radio, newspapers, digital-first outlets, and broadcast and cable television, with our aim of creating a replicable approach to corpus construction, even in light of challenges such as for-profit library databases, limitations in Google indexing, and online archiving of television. More details about our corpus construction can be found in Online Appendix B. Citations for the stories drawn from our corpus that are referenced in the main text can be found in a separate reference list in Online Appendix C.

In Section 3, The Context and Structure for Illinois' Political and Media Ecosystems, we address our first research question about the political ecologies that enable the rise of extremist politicians. Specifically, we discuss the structural and cultural elements of the politics and media ecosystems that create opportunistic conditions for capture by extremist politicians, especially on the right, and draw on interview data for additional context to understand on-the-ground political dynamics.

In Section 4, The Rise of Darren Bailey: PMP and the Political Economy of the News Industry, we further refine our second research question and ask: "How (and why) did the coverage of Bailey evolve to set up his national breakthrough and set his political career in motion? We draw on our extended timeline (in Online Appendix A) and our media corpus (see Online Appendix B) to inform our analysis. We further operationalize our second research question through two additional departure points:

1. Media structure: using the corpus and the structure of the news ecology to understand the dynamics within the coverage – both temporally and across different news media and categories of sources
2. News norms: using text from the corpus to consider how the coverage itself may have facilitated the accidental amplification of Bailey and his extremist politics

This analysis illustrates how the structural and normative dimensions of American journalism contributed to the amplification of Bailey's persona.

In Section 6, Avoiding Accidental Amplification, we provide an overview of the key empirical contributions from our scholarship. We reckon with the contradictions of the normative democratic obligation of the press to inform, the political economy of the contemporary US news media, and the challenges of confronting the rise of nationalist populism in the hyperpolarized, politically fraught political culture in the US.

While generalizing across all would-be local extremists from this case is not possible, this case study surfaces concerns that have wider relevance for political communication, not just in the US but globally: rural versus urban tensions, the radicalization of the right-wing, and the interplay of local, state, and national, partisan news media in a time of heightened economic instability in the news industry and rising political extremism. Ultimately, we hope that this work can encourage stakeholders, scholars, and journalists alike to exercise due caution: ordinary routines and norms of press/politics are insufficient for extraordinary times like the present, when there is a real and present danger of democratic backsliding.

1 Theorizing Extremist Politicians and the Democratic Press

Is Bailey an extremist if his views reflect the now-dominant positions of the Republican party in the wake of the 2024 election? Given that he used the court system to challenge emergency powers, is it fair to call his politics illiberal or antidemocratic? Even if his springboard into state political power adhered to the rule of law, can we point to his growing power and influence as evidence of democratic backsliding?

We have wrestled with how to define Bailey and his brand of politics. Many public stakeholders argue that democratic processes can be used to unravel democratic norms and platform illiberal politics – the *sine qua non* being the Trump administration itself. Democracy, as a civil religion – what Bellah (1967) describes as the awareness of "the responsibility and the significance our republican experiment has for the whole world" (p. 16) – demands a certain wager based on faith in institutions we know to be imperfect. These include the existence of free and fair elections, the peaceful transfer of power, the importance of free speech and the press, and adherence to the democratically enacted rule of law. Others would go further and suggest that democracy disintegrates when there is no longer mutual tolerance – respect for disagreement and diminished institutional forbearance – or respect for the rule of law (Levitsky & Ziblatt, 2018).

In this Element, we have decided to use the word "extremist" to describe Bailey because his views were very far from the pro-business, libertarian, and largely a-religious Republicanism that has characterized Illinois Republican politics since the 1970s (Pearson & Gorner, 2024). We also argue that he later used this new power to create a space for illiberal politics and modeled them through his own actions and public pronouncements: casting doubt on the 2020 election results; refusing to mask in the Illinois State House despite rules requiring him to do so; promising to defy any bans on assault weapons; jokes about jailing Pritzker, and beyond.

Bailey's actions during early COVID led the way for additional officials to defy Pritzker's orders; garnering him support from protestors marching against COVID restrictions, some of whom used their own extreme language likening Pritzker to Nazis. Bailey's brand of Republicanism is at this point the standard-bearer national Republican platform, anti-choice, progun, anti-elite, anti-urban, Christian conservatism is no longer extreme. Pritzker may have labeled him "too extreme for Illinois" in their gubernatorial battle (Meisel, 2022), but Bailey is anything but in terms of national politics. Even so, we believe that it is accurate to characterize Bailey's brand of politics, at least during the time that we are analyzing it, as extreme; and we argue that this form of extremism has been central to the rise of illiberalism in US politics as well.

Certainly, democratic processes can be used for illiberal/antidemocratic ends, but it is important to remember that resistance to the rule of law/the spirit of the law has also catalyzed opposition that has widely been seen on the side of justice. Normatively, we believe that reliance on the wheels of democratic processes is not a blank check for advancing political positions that question those very same democratic norms. Historically, we know that democratic processes have legitimized the rise of autocrats like Hitler and more recently, Victor Orban, and closer to home, have given the force of law in the US for racist, immoral segregation policies. Right-wing populism is indeed cresting, raising real concerns for women's rights, LGBTQ+ rights, protections for other minorities, and Democrats more generally. Whether rollbacks of these progressive gains simply reflect how empowered Republicans govern or the assault on mutual tolerance and institutional forbearance remains unclear.

Nonetheless, this Element does have the benefit of hindsight, as it was written almost five years after the events and media coverage we so closely detail here. It is traumatic for us as authors to think about the uncertain and scary first days of the pandemic. But, it is important to remember just how little we knew about COVID, how underequipped hospitals were with ventilators, and how shocking it was for the world to essentially come to a halt. At the same time, we now know that many COVID policies and advisories may indeed have been wrongheaded, ineffective, or unscientific: from closing schools (Mervoush, Miller & Paris, 2024) to shoddy cloth masking practices (Zeilinger, 2023) to the six-foot social distancing rule (Diamond, 2024). Fundamentally, Bailey's springboard into public consciousness was his resistance to Pritzker's COVID emergency order. Indeed, this is a microstudy of one small town politician. However, this case is exemplary of the playbook that unknown backbenchers and community activists use to gain prominence, thanks to both enduring weaknesses in journalistic practices and the contemporary pathologies of the market failure of contemporary journalism.

Before discussing the theoretical framework for our research and the methodological approach, we offer the following abbreviated scene-setting and timeline to help ground the case, which showcases Bailey's meteoric accumulation of political influence and media attention (for the more extensive outline, see Online Appendix A).

1.1 The Early COVID-19 Response in Illinois

On March 9, 2020, with eleven reported cases in the state, Democratic Governor J. B. Pritzker declared a disaster proclamation over the COVID-19 pandemic, the state's version of a "state of emergency," granting the governor authority "to transfer the direction, personnel or functions of State departments and agencies or units thereof for the purpose of performing or facilitating emergency response programs," from the Illinois' Board of Education to the Illinois Department of Public Health (NBC Chicago, 2020). On March 21, 2020, Pritzer announced a "stay at home order," (Executive Order 2020–10) citing the rapid spread of COVID-19 throughout the state and the need to ensure that "the healthcare delivery system is capable of serving those who are sick." Pritzker's stay-at-home order, what is colloquially referred to as "lockdown," at the time prohibited all "non-essential business and operations," with residents directed to "stay at home or at their place of residence" except for the reasons outlined in the order and schools across the state ordered to close (Pritzker, 2020, March 20). The initial stay-at-home order was through April 7, but on March 31, Pritzker announced that it would be extended to include the entire month of April ("Illinois Stay-at-Home Order," 2020).

1.2 Bailey's Rise: April 23 to May 2, 2020

In this section, we provide a brief, day-by-day overview of the legal actions and media coverage of Bailey's lawsuit challenging the stay-at-home order. For each day, we describe actions by political actors, as well as summarize the extent of the coverage that day at both the local and national levels.

1.2.1 Thursday, April 23

On Thursday, April 23, 2020, Pritzker announced that he would sign a new stay-at-home order, effective through the month of May. The new order (Executive Order 2020–32) allowed the reopening of garden centers, golf courses, and state parks and permitted elective surgeries and pickup or delivery retail services. The new order also mandated masks for everyone over the age of two in any location where six-foot social distancing could not be maintained (*Pritzker Breaks Down Changes*, 2020).

State Senator Darren Bailey filed a complaint in Clay County circuit court against Pritzker, asking for an injunction to overturn the executive order, claiming that it undermined his civil rights. Bailey's hometown of Xenia, population 384, is in Clay County and had only two reported COVID cases at the time. Via Facebook Live and mobile video, Bailey stood in front of the Clay County Court House, proclaiming "Enough is enough! I filed this lawsuit on behalf of myself and my constituents who are ready to go back to work and resume a normal life." Two local television stations also covered the announcement and linked to the Facebook Live video: WAND, which serves the Champaign and Springfield media markets, and WSIL, which reaches southern

Illinois, southeast Missouri, western Kentucky, and northwestern Tennessee, shared news of the suit. Nationally, the AP picked up the story, which was republished with a different headline by the conservative *Washington Times*.[1] Bailey shared this story on his Facebook page, calling it "national news."

Total coverage: twelve stories (two national, ten local)

1.2.2 Friday, April 24

Bailey held a press conference via Facebook Live to provide journalists with more details about his lawsuit. Pritzker responded to a question about the lawsuit during his daily COVID briefing, telling journalists, "Frankly, I think that a lawsuit about whether or not this is an emergency is a political maneuver." The lawsuit is covered in the *Chicago Tribune*, by *Capitol News Illinois,* the state political news nonprofit, *Politico*, and the right-wing *Washington Examiner*. The lawsuit is also covered in the Gannett-owned *State Journal Register*, *NPR Illinois*, the NPR (Northern Public Radio) station headquartered in Springfield (capital of Illinois).

Total coverage: eleven stories (one national, ten local)

1.2.3 Saturday, April 25 and Sunday, April 26

Pritzker's response to Bailey from the 24th fuels most of the weekend's coverage of activity in the Illinois State House. Bailey appeared on "Capitol Connection," a statewide television show produced by Nexstar Media, a television conglomerate out of Springfield. The *Capitol Fax* blog accuses Bailey of causing the conflict for personal gain and attention, which may have also helped direct additional reporting attention by other outlets to the emerging conflict.

Total coverage: April 25 (fourteen local) and April 26 (six local)

1.2.4 Monday, April 27

Clay County Circuit Court Judge Michael McHaney, a Republican judge, issued a temporary restraining order against Pritzker, ruling Pritzker could not force Bailey to isolate and quarantine. His decision refers to Pritzker as having "shredded the Constitution." However, the ruling only applied to Bailey, not to other state residents.

Both the AP and Reuters covered the story. Within Illinois, coverage of the ruling exploded: Bailey appeared in *Politico's* Illinois Playbook in the "Top Talker" section at the top of the email newsletter. *The Chicago Sun-Times*, and

---

[1] The Associated Press is a cooperative of news organizations. AP members are allowed to use AP content.

the *Chicago Tribune* published stories about the lawsuit, as did local television stations and another local NPR station. Chicago's PBS station, WTTW, interviewed Bailey and promoted a link to an extended nineteen-minute video on its website. The case is mentioned in digital-first hyperlocal outlets in places such as the *Evanston Round Table, Block Club Chicago*, and in Patch's *Illinois* news roundup. Right-wing media outlets covering the decision include the *Washington Times, The Daily Caller, Breitbart*, and the *Gateway Pundit*.

Total coverage: eighty-five stories (seventy-five local, ten national/international)

1.2.5 Tuesday, April 28

The Illinois Attorney General filed notice of an appeal against Bailey, which moved the lawsuit to the state's Fifth Appellate Court. Pritzker directed his attention to Bailey in his daily press briefing, calling his actions a "cheap political stunt designed so that the representative can see his name in headlines, and unfortunately, he has briefly been successful in that most callous of feats."

The story received its peak national coverage on April 28, with articles in the *Washington Post,* CNN (web only), NPR (web only), and the AP. Local coverage included: The *Sun-Times,* five stories in the *Chicago Tribune* (including a critical editorial), and Chicago's *WGN Radio* also hosted Bailey for a twelve-minute interview with its midday host. On the right, the *Washington Examiner, The Washington Times,* and a California-focused right-wing blog, Right On Daily Blog covered the story.

Total coverage: 115 (97 local, 18 national/international)

1.2.6 Wednesday, April 29

On April 29, Pritzker revised the stay-at-home extension to give nonessential businesses the ability to open to the public for curbside pickup. Richland County Tuberculosis and Public Health Office announced that a COVID-19-positive resident of Bailey's district has violated Pritzker's order. The COVID-positive resident is described as visiting CVS, Walmart, and a gas station the day prior.

Bailey was a guest on Laura Ingraham's *Ingraham Angle* for a 3:25 minute spot as Fox News shows saw pandemic-fueled growth in ratings – April 2020 was the network's most-watched month ever in prime time, with Ingraham's audience averaging 3.6 million viewers – (Katz, 2020). The case also garnered coverage in *The Daily Wire* and *Breitbart.* The *Chicago Tribune* published four stories and republished another.

Total coverage: 158 stories (149 local, 9 national/international)

1.2.7 Thursday, April 30

The co-chair of Trump's reelection campaign in Illinois filed another lawsuit, intended to be on behalf of all residents. A northern Illinois church also filed suit against Pritzker in federal court over his extended stay-at-home order, claiming that Pritzker is "hostile" to those exercising their religion. The same day, however, the stay-at-home order was modified to allow worship gatherings of limited size (Ayres-Brown & Petrella, 2020). Bailey asked the Fifth Appellate Court to vacate the restraining order, saying he would refile the lawsuit.

The day after his Fox appearance, Bailey won an institutional Republican media capstone: the right-leaning opinion page of the *Wall Street Journal* (WSJ) featured a contribution heralding Bailey's bravery. Other coverage includes a *USA Today* roundup of newsworthy events happening across all fifty states and *The Daily Mail*. State and local television outlets and newspapers reported on the quarantine violation, noting that the COVID-positive resident was in Bailey's district. The *New York Times* referenced the lawsuit without naming Bailey directly.

Total coverage: eighty-eight (eighty-two local, six national/international)

1.2.8 Friday, May 1

Two "Re-open Illinois" rallies are hosted, one in Springfield, the other in Chicago. In Chicago, a protester holds the sign, "'Arbeit macht frei', JB" a phrase from the infamous sign from the Nazi extermination camp, Auschwitz. Another protester displayed a "Heil Pritzker" sign. Similar signs are seen in Springfield. Pritzker is Jewish. The larger story begins to move beyond Bailey, although the *Chicago Tribune* runs four stories mentioning him. The AP covered the rallies, while *Capitol News Illinois* wrote about Bailey's request to vacate.

Total coverage: seventy-eight (seventy-four local, four national/international)

1.2.9 Saturday, May 2

National news coverage of COVID in Illinois focused on the protests. *The New York Times* mentioned protests against Pritzker but not Bailey or the lawsuit. *Buzzfeed News* collated tweets with evidence of the Nazi protest signs in an article "A woman at an Anti-Lockdown protest held a sign from a Nazi concentration camp." *Forbes* and *The Guardian* also covered the protests. Other outlets will go on cover the protest over the following days, including *Business Insider* (May 3), ABC network news and beyond, as the focus turns to the unacceptable nature of the Nazi and Holocaust-linked language.

Total coverage: twenty-nine (twenty-six local, three national/international)

1.3 Theorizing the Jump-Start of a Small Town Extremist

The main takeaway from this abbreviated timeline is this: in under a week, a first-term state representative in the minority party from a small, rural town managed to end up on one of Fox News' biggest shows – jump-starting his state and national political career. But Bailey's path needs to be understood within a materially situated political and media context; tracking the content of news stories alone offers an incomplete understanding of the opportunistic conditions for the emergence of empowered extremist politicians. Whether politics influences the media or media sets the tone and structure for politics can be debated, both theoretically and empirically. To this end, we turn first to the Politics-Media-Politics (PMP) approach as a useful conceptual map to chart how the mature digital and legacy right-wing media ecosystem and how an increasingly anemic local news media creates opportunities for political extremism to flourish. We also combine two other literatures to help with the inductive process of understanding how and why news media coverage evolved: first, the literature on media storms, or when journalists pursue a storyline with a sudden intensity of media attention that then peters out to similar levels of coverage of related issues or events (Boydstun, Hardy & Walgrave, 2014); and second, political economy scholarship on journalism, which brings together an understanding of how journalism's professional norms and cultures are situated in a larger structural context where flows of information depend on ownership, economic pressure, and other institutional and cultural constraints. By uniting these strands of scholarly literature, we situate our case study of how small town politicians are able to take advantage of the news industry and polarize local and state politics to stratospherically rise in reputation and name recognition.

1.3.1 Politics-Media-Politics

Developed by Wolfsfeld (2013; Wolfsfeld, Segev & Sheafer, 2013) and then extended in various empirical and theoretical scholarly contributions, most fully in Wolfsfeld, Sheafer & Althaus (2022),[2] the PMP approach is an interpretive framework that aims to integrate analysis of media *and* analysis of politics. The PMP framework conceives of politics and communication as ecosystems; the political ecosystem "centers on the ongoing competition over influence and power that are central to politics" while the communication ecosystem is defined as focusing on all individuals and organizations (not just professionals) "involved in producing, distributing, and validating all of these different forms of communication" (Wolfsfeld, Sheafer & Althaus, 2022).

---

[2] This summary of the PMP approach is primarily drawn from the first chapter of Wolfsfeld, Sheafer & Althaus (2022, specifically p. 6–29 and Table 1.2). Critiques of the approach itself are best addressed by the authors' monograph'.

This PMP ecosystem approach helps contextualize social science in society, such that it accounts for structure, culture, and temporality. The first proposition is that "politics" come first: the underlying political ecosystem sets into motion how the media system responds. The structural level of the political ecosystem consists of long-term institutional rules and norms that shape governance, such as the electoral system. The cultural level of a political ecosystem is more contextual and "medium term," reflecting both aggregate and collective values, beliefs, norms, and actions of political actors, for example, the level of political consensus or extremism. The second principle of PMP is that media do not simply reflect politics, but they can also have an independent effect on political processes through the selection and transformation of events and issues into stories (p.16). The media ecosystem similarly consists of three levels of analysis; the structural level is the long-term features of the ecosystem that influence *all* forms of media in a particular time and place, examples of which include press freedom, the economic foundation of the media, and the underlying technological infrastructure. The cultural factors include the values, beliefs, and actions among what Wolfsfeld et al. broadly describe as "content producers" about the "collection, construction, transmission, and veracity of political stories within a particular time and place" (p. 18). For example, this includes sensationalism or the culture of investigative journalism. For both media and political ecosystems, the situational level analysis is short term and includes "major events or circumstances" that shape political activity, and in turn, the creation, construction, production, and transmission of political information – for example, a natural disaster, a political scandal, a spike in digital political discourse such as #metoo, or in this case, the beginning of the COVID-19. PMP, then, is politics first, followed by media, which in turn, shapes politics, either structurally, culturally, or situationally, or some combination of all three. Wolfsfeld et al. (2022) acknowledge that there have been decades of scholars who have considered media production, content creation, and consumption to understand the "effect" of media, broadly described. The advantage of the PMP approach is that these questions are bound up in direct conversation with the political ecosystem that surrounds the context of media – and more specifically, directs importance to how journalism is both shaped and structured by *where* it is culturally, geographically, and politically situated (Usher, 2021). Thus, given that our interest was in the rapid ascent of Bailey in a matter of days, we turned to this framework to situate the context of the political and media ecosystem that created a runway for his rise.

1.3.2 Sudden Burst of Media Attention: Media Storms

If the first step to structuring our research was to understand the underlying political and media contexts, a closer look at media storms scholarship gives us both vocabulary and insights to help answer our second research question, about how journalism itself – both the profession's practices and norms and the structure of the contemporary news industry itself – might in turn amplify extremism. More specifically, looking at aggregate coverage patterns across the unfolding political events enables a descriptive disentangling of Bailey's massive national breakthrough which set Bailey's political career in motion beyond representing his county of 13,000 in the Illinois State House. Looking at the ebbs and flows in media attention provides the zoomed-out picture of *how and why* this coverage emerged (which in turn guides our later interpretive, grounded-theory approach to the corpus analysis).

Boydstun, Hardy & Walgrave (2014) developed the concept of "media storms" as a way to explain surges in media attention, when "news outlets often become suddenly and strongly riveted to a storyline" and devote "sudden, high, and sustained media attention to an event or issue" (p. 509). As they explain, this rapid onset of media attention might sometimes be explained by an event (for example, a natural disaster or news of a shocking scandal), but in other cases, the interest appears somewhat random: there might be many other incidents of the same behavior or action happening but news media focus on just one, elevating it to heightened significance and attention for a brief period. Boydstun and colleagues (2014; Walgrave et al., 2017) find that most news coverage of issues has a more punctuated equilibrium pattern, "the day-to-day change in media attention oscillates explosively between almost no change at all and extreme change" (2014, p. 510), and this maps on, generally, to overall patterns in policy discussions writ large.

However, media storms look different: instead of the punctuated equilibrium-style bursts of more routine news coverage, there is a Gaussian/normal distribution of coverage. After repeated studies, including over eleven years of US and cross-national data, as well as "four million newspaper articles in seventy years of coverage in the Dutch newspaper *De Telegraaf*" (Hardy, 2017, p. 26), this distribution appears regardless of the content itself (Walgrave et al., 2017). These scholars developed a three-part definition for assessing the presence of a media storm: explosiveness or a surge in attention, size or the volume of coverage, and duration, which the authors point to as a "significant period" at least in terms of how much time journalists generally focus on one particular issue or subject (Walgrave et al., 2017, p. 556). Across this work, media storm scholars argue that the phenomenon is both multimodal, that is across different types of media, and also reflects the intermedia agenda-setting among news outlets.

However, these media storms also may distort and amplify news coverage (Vasterman, 2005), both reflecting and refracting preexisting structural, normative, and institutional challenges that scholars have identified as falling short of more optimal coverage that might better inform the public. Hardy (2017) considers how diminished gatekeeping and news imitation might contribute to the conditions for creating a media storm: first, a key event can cause an increase in coverage of the event itself, lowering the barrier of newsworthiness for coverage about topically similar events, and different news organizations may simultaneously choose to cover this event. The tendency of news organizations to imitate other news organizations further contributes to the intensity of coverage, but as news organizations compete in the attention economy for web traffic, this competitive impulse may also make other news values such as newsworthiness or relevance less important (Usher, 2014, 2018).

Moreover, in the US, the growing nationalization of local news and politics means that local political issues are often framed in terms of national ones and increasingly mirror the partisan positions held nationally (Hopkins, 2018). While the empirical evidence of media storms is rich, these storms have thus far been understood as about issues or events rather than personalities, and it is unclear just how politicians might benefit from the rapid onset of media attention. Some scholars argue that politicians strategically use these moments of intense coverage to advance their political agendas (Elmelund-Praestekaer & Wien, 2008). However, others argue that politicians appear more vulnerable to the media leading the agenda (Gruszczynski, 2020). But Dumouchel (2023) finds evidence that for specific electoral contexts, political parties might find these media storms opportunistic, particularly if there is little political risk to their engagement – on the other hand, however, individual politicians may be less able to take advantage of them.

As a whole, neither PMP nor media storm research considers the downstream impact on the larger political ecology, especially one that has become deeply politically polarized, and rarely situates this work within local and regional geography. PMP and media storms have also largely been applied to a universe where politicians follow traditional political norms and democratic values that have remained fairly consistent in press/politics for most of the US postwar era. To complete the theoretical and empirical grounding for this case study, we offer a brief overview from the scholarship in the political economy of journalism.

1.3.3 News Media and Political Economy

A brief overview of journalistic norms and the state of the US news industry helps explain how journalistic practices may contribute to amplifying extremist politicians and create an opening for illiberalism by failing to adequately cover the magnitude of the threat posed to democracy. The institutional news media, or the "mainstream news media" is composed of journalists and news organizations who see themselves as part of a profession that adheres to standards and ethics of fact-based, verified news gathering. Since the late 1960s, US journalism has favored an "objective" approach to covering politics, which in theory is a methodology for asking questions and weighing evidence (Kovach & Rosenstiel, 2021). However, scholars have long maligned how a commitment to objectivity in practice can result in false balance – overemphasizing perspectives and politics that may have proportionally less support. Journalistic commitment to objectivity also centers neutrality and impartiality as important components of journalistic autonomy and independence; professional journalists imagine that approach enables them to stand back from making direct judgments of ongoing events, a detachment believed to facilitate reporting facts rather than opinions (Örnebring & Karlsson, 2022). However, this commitment to neutrality is not realistic: journalists make decisions all the time about what to cover and not to cover and how to frame stories. Scholars argue that the "view from nowhere" approach to journalism can be problematic, leaving the public without normative guidance about how to interpret the significance of ongoing events and power struggles in public life (Rosen, 1999).

Professional journalism's normative commitment to objectivity has also made it vulnerable to media manipulation by antidemocratic politicians and political causes. By repeating false claims or centering illiberal politics as part of story construction, news organizations can inadvertently amplify these ideas and their proponents. While we do not know how intentionally Bailey took advantage of this normative vulnerability, a wide range of antidemocratic bad actors do strategically engage in media manipulation (Marwick & Lewis, 2017). As per Wagner (2007), the two-party system in the US means that journalists can balance the amount of coverage of each party, enabling extremist views to be couched as inter-party differences. Neutral coverage of democratic backsliding, approached with objectivity norms in mind, can end up empowering antidemocratic actors and threats to political institutions (Carlson, Robinson & Lewis, 2021; Karlsson, Ferrer Conill & Örnebring, 2023).

The institutional news media's defense of their work as objective may be compounded by ideological capture. In light of the continued, national GOP effort to paint the mainstream news as liberal, most Americans believe that journalists present a liberal view of the world (Watts et al., 1999; Hassel, Holbein & Miles, 2020). In turn, this may prompt journalists to overproduce stenographic, uncritical coverage as a defensive strategy to avoid accusations of media bias, especially from Republicans (Usher, 2019). During the 2016 and 2020 elections and to the present, both *The New York Times* and *Washington Post* insisted upon their own impartiality and pointed to their heightened scrutiny of all candidates. As then-*Washington Post* editor Marty Baron put it in early 2017, "The way I view it is, we're not at war with the administration, we're at work. We're doing our jobs." More recently, *New York Times* executive editor Joe Kahn explained:

> If we become a partisan organization exclusively focused on threats to democracy, and we give up our coverage of the issues, the social, political, and cultural divides that are animating participation in politics in America, we will lose the battle to be independent. Underscoring that it was unreasonable to expect an objective newspaper to serve this role (Barr, 2022).

By covering what Trump said and did, with limited additional context for readers, listeners, or viewers, fact-driven, "straight" news reports that aimed to provide reports of the day did just that – but critics argue those reports of the day included white nationalist, anti-institutionalist rhetoric, misinformation, and attacks on democratic norms. This journalistic detachment might have made sense in the past, but this effort to remain impartial may actually imperil American democracy itself by failing to inform the public of the dangerous surge in extremist politicians. Unfortunately, the ordinary coverage of extremist politics has been good for the bottom lines of national news organizations, resulting in a "Trump bump" for ratings and subscriptions. As the now-disgraced former CBS CEO Les Moonves said in 2016, "It may not be good for America, but it's damn good for CBS" (Collins, 2016).

1.3.4 News Norms and News Distortions

Journalism norms favor coverage of the unexpected and novel, gravitate towards sensationalism, and result in routine coverage of knowns (Gans, 1979/2004). For decades, scholars have pointed to problems with national political coverage, from journalists' preference for horse race coverage (Searles & Banda, 2019), to a focus on personality-driven stories and so-called "palace intrigue," the need for access/source reliance, false neutrality, and beyond for falling short of optimal coverage of politics (Entman, 2004; Bennett, Lawrence & Livingston, 2008). Carey (1997), Cook (2012), and others have observed that both journalists and Americans engage with politics as an unfolding drama of conflict, good and bad actors, scandal, and moral failings, in part because this is how narrative structure shapes stories, and in part because this is what makes the otherwise dry and shapeless gavel-to-gavel, event-to-event coverage of politics simply more interesting.

While there is substantial media fragmentation, the large national, institutional news media outlets continue to play a gatekeeping role when it comes to coverage of political elites, deciding who and what gets covered. A study of cable and broadcast coverage of the US House found that more extreme politicians on both sides of the aisle were "vastly overrepresented" when compared to their mainline counterparts – with the effect of making the House seem more polarized than it actually is (Padgett et al., 2019, p. 609). Other work suggests that extreme Republicans were more likely to get coverage than extreme Democrats – and that journalists cover extremists because journalists know "news audiences like a good fight" and because extreme partisans may be more likely to make statements about various legislative proposals (Wagner & Gruszczynski, 2018). Certainly, Americans may be growing more ideologically polarized – with acute shifts in affective polarization, such that their assessment of out-group partisans has become more negative than at any point in postwar America (Mason, 2018). But the nationalization of American *attention* to the news is its own form of polarization (Darr, Hitt & Dunaway, 2021), and this in turn may lead local and state-level politicians to try to align more with national party concerns and issues (Hopkins, 2018).

Others have demonstrated how "pink slime" news outlets funded by shadowy Republican backers who fail to disclose their partisan ties may also be distorting local news ecosystems. During the period under study, Bailey did not appear on the biggest network of these pink slime sites once, although received considerable amplification in local news ecosystems through these sites during his 2022 gubernatorial campaign (Wenzel et al., 2023). Scholars in Wisconsin have found that politically interested citizens with less access to local news are increasingly turning to national partisan sources, especially on the right (Wells et al., 2021). These developments are particularly concerning for the media ecology at the local and regional level, which is facing the most dire and dramatic contractions.

1.3.5 Economic Pressure, Local, and National News

Structural challenges to the news industry compound these normative professional constraints, especially as tech companies guzzle audience attention and ad revenue away from news organizations. Newspapers have long provided the bulk of original news content about any one place, the "keystone" media providing the foundation for television, radio, and digital content alike (Nielsen, 2015). Hayes and Lawless (2021) estimate the volume of local political news, defined as coverage of mayors, city and town councils, local school boards, and city governments, has dropped by more than 56 percent from 1997 to 2017 (pp. 26–27), while other estimates of the effects of declines in newspaper staffing at large regional dailies suggest that newspapers produce between 300 and 500 fewer political stories each year (Peterson, 2021). Across the

US, approximately 1,800 communities have lost access to a regular supply of professionally produced local news (Abernathy, 2020); other estimates from the Northwestern Local News Initiative suggest more than 55 million Americans may have limited to no access to local news (including 206 counties without any local news sources at all) (Metzger, 2024). As investment owners and hedge funds have gobbled up news organizations as distressed assets, on average, newsrooms have lost nine reporters and editors, or about 14 percent of the average newspaper's staff – mostly in general assignment and political reporting (Peterson & Dunaway, 2023). Newspapers are simply producing less original local news.

This case study focuses on a state house representative. Diminished state house coverage might further challenge more local and state-focused coverage of state politics. As a whole, newspaper coverage of state houses has declined (Abernathy, 2020), although some state house journalism has been augmented by nonprofit interventions and the rise of niche digital-first outlets like *Politico* and *Axios*. If national news outlets face challenges covering threats to democracy, more local threats to democratic institutions may be even harder to address, as local news outlets often lack the resources, skills, and potentially, the audience interest to alert communities to these dangers. Regional news outlets, especially big city dailies, have cut back their statewide coverage. Constrained by the "goldilocks" audience problem of being too large to generate niche local audiences that favor targeted advertising but not big enough to garner national attention, these newspapers have continued to contract their staff and their audiences (Usher, 2021). In many cases, small community newspapers have focused on community cohesion rather than aggressive investigative journalism about local businesses and institutions, leaving these local news outlets reluctant to focus on coverage of contentious issues (Carey, 2017). Despite the challenges across all sectors of the American news industry, there has been little scholarly research focused on how these changes in the news industry intersect with the rise of extremist politics at the state and local levels. This leaves gaps in our understanding of how the institutional news media covers candidates and politicians who do not yet have a national (or even state) reputation.

2 Methodology: The Case Study Corpus

Our approach pushes the boundaries of political communication methodology through our qualitative case-study approach at the *micro* level – one individual politician's rise over one particular, defined temporal range. While much of quantitative political communication abstracts individual or case-study approaches in search of more generalizable findings, a qualitative case-study approach is helpful for teasing out the dynamics of ongoing phenomena, giving a sense of the stakes of the research within a situated, material context. Herbst (1998) argues that power and politics need to be understood as constructed within local environments and contexts, signaling the importance of beginning with close microstudies to help identify broader departure points for quantitative research favoring generalizability. Others have suggested that an empirical examination of the micro level can help to surface agonistic and antidemocratic tensions (Karppinen, Moe & Svensson, 2008).

Personifying the rise of extremism, quite literally through the trajectory of a single previously unknown politician, offers an affective dimension that can get lost in a larger discourse about national politics and political trends. As Markham et al. (2021) argue, "the granular or microscopic practices of everyday life and inquiry" also connect back up with the "massive scales and macroscopic aspects of this moment in time." They argue this approach is well-suited for thinking about moments of crisis, such as the COVID pandemic, which offers generative potential from which to consider more macro and systemic scholarly questions. In addition, a focus on Illinois is warranted. Previous Element contributions have considered communication ecologies within the context of Wisconsin – another Midwestern state with a far more "purple" political dynamic than Illinois (Friedland et al., 2022). Illinois, however, is a far more reliably "blue" state, and as such, its underlying political dynamics set up Republican politicians and the rural areas that they represent as marginalized political opponents with little hope for meaningful statewide political power.

2.1 Data Gathering and Corpus Construction

A mixed method approach stimulated the main research questions, with the lead author engaging in fieldwork embedded in the downstate Illinois Republican party beginning in August 2020 and ending in August 2022. Both authors, as residents of rural Illinois, observed Bailey's ascent in real time and our initial research questions emerged from more observational and anecdotal data. The second and primary method for this paper was to reconstruct a ten-day period between Thursday, April 23, and Sunday, May 2, 2020, to more closely examine Bailey's breakthrough on Fox News; this ten-day period was chosen because it reflects the most immediate movement of the case and the state government's response, but it is also bookended by a right-wing nationalist protest event against the lockdown.

Between January 2021 and August 2022, the first author led a research team at the University of Illinois Urbana-Champaign focused on community information needs and democratic politics, the PPLN-IL group (Platforms, Politics, and Local News in Illinois). This research team used the COVID-19 pandemic to spark a larger research project about how diminished local professional news ecologies and the augmented role of platforms like Facebook were impacting rural communities in Illinois (Usher, 2022, 2023; Usher et al., 2023). The first author engaged in an interview-based project of rural public health officials and also conducted fieldwork facilitated through a partnership with a longtime Illinois Republican political strategist and former political science professor, Jim Nowlan. Field observations with Nowlan included two private dinners that served as pseudo-focus groups with key informants: civic leaders, political party organizers, journalists, and business owners, and attendance at a Kiwanis meeting. The author also observed two media meet-and-greet events prior to the pandemic with the Champaign-Urbana NPR member station, WILL, and the Champaign-Urbana daily newspaper, *The News-Gazette*. They conducted interviews with local farmers, local journalists working for both independent and institutional news media, and local civic activists.

While this background helps set up the case itself and enables a more textured interpretation of our corpus, the media corpus we created serves as the centerpiece for our specific research questions in this Element. For our corpus, we deployed a two-pronged approach to locating relevant media coverage over the ten-day period, combining systematic searches of aggregate news databases (provided by the authors' university libraries) and web search tools with targeted searching of news sources based on the authors' knowledge of relevant local, regional and partisan news sources that covered Bailey's lawsuit.

2.2 Collecting News Stories

To create our corpus, the first and second authors took the approach illustrated in Figure 1, combining aggregate search tools such as open and proprietary news databases, and targeted searches of news outlets and digital platforms for the

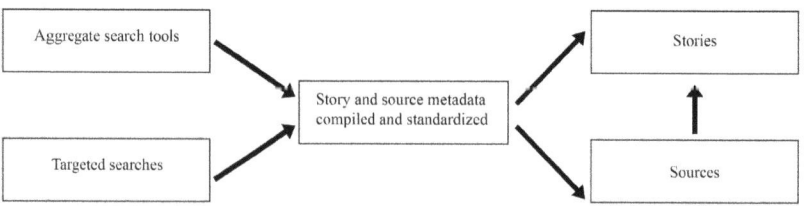

Figure 1 Illustration of the data collection and analysis process.

search term "Darren Bailey" from April 23 to May 2, 2020. Our total corpus consisted of 596 non-duplicated stories across 126 newspapers, TV programming, radio broadcasts, wire, and digital-first sources. This corpus can be found online as a supplemental file www.cambridge.org/Usher.

Indexed news content providers included Access World News (Newsbank Inc.), Nexis Uni (Lexis Nexis), and Factiva (Dow Jones). In Access World News, we searched for the keyword phrase "Darren Bailey" in all text of newspaper sources located in Illinois and all broadcast transcripts. In Nexis Uni and Factiva, we used the same keyword searches for all newspaper content. In all three databases, we limited the search results to the study time period (April 23 to May 2, 2020) and exported results as PDF documents. To build our corpus of television coverage, we used Internet Archive's TV News Archive. In order to address possible gaps in the archive's metadata, we also searched for "Pritzker" and "lawsuit" during our time frame. Student researchers then watched all the clips, summarized them, and indicated whether Bailey was mentioned by name; as we were interested in Bailey's rise, our focus was on content that specifically mentioned him by name, rather than more oblique references by Pritzker and in news coverage.

We also searched for Bailey's name in a time-limited search on Google News, Meta's Crowdtangle, and Twitter (now known as X). Web searches returned stories that we added to the corpus as well as suggesting news sources we used in our targeted searches. The Google Advanced Search terms were specifically delineated for "Darren Bailey," but because Google News' archiving practices are black-boxed, we extended the dates to include April 23, 2020, and May 5, 2020. We used the same search strings on four different computers and with three different Google email accounts to account for potential differences in search results. This search, conducted in San Diego, likely surfaced national content first, given the distance between San Diego and Illinois (Jadika et al., 2023); however, the first author and two student assistants logged every search result in a spreadsheet. If the sources from Google News were not already included in the databases, we then did targeted searches of these sources on their webpages. This was particularly important for obtaining content from local television and smaller digital-first websites. The Crowdtangle search found that the total interactions for "Darren Bailey" across public Facebook pages was 78,536 interactions across 495 public posts, with the distribution of interactions peaking on April 28, 2020, with 41.8 k interactions. Our social media searches through Crowdtangle and Twitter from April 23, 2020, and May 5, 2020, only returned three public posts with mentions of two different sources that we did not already have in our corpus, both referencing a country music stations local to Bailey's district.

As we could not recover the text or audio for these broadcasts, we did not include them in our corpus. Notably, other scholars have found that music stations in rural locales offer only brief mentions of local political news and information (Friedland et al., 2022), and as the broadcast audience included Bailey's constituents, we do not see this as a missing component to understanding his growing public footprint. Social media undoubtedly became a more important aspect of Bailey's growing political career as time continued. Public engagement on social media about Bailey was not the focus of our research as we were most concerned with the role of news media and the interrelationship between press/politics. Other than references to Bailey's Facebook Live posts, the news coverage in our corpus does not reference any of his Twitter posts or any social media activity among the general public.

2.3 Story and Source Analysis

The second author, with support from undergraduate research assistants, compiled all of the identified stories into a data set on which we conducted a descriptive quantitative analysis to answer the study questions. This produced two sets of data: stories and sources. The initial data set includes 651 news stories identified through our search of aggregate search tools and targeted searches of relevant publications. Sources refer to the publication outlets, such as newspapers, conservative news sites, and television or radio stations. For each source, we collected the following metadata: publication title, type of search (aggregate vs targeted), medium, geographic category, and type of source. The source data related to medium, geography, and source type were linked to the stories data set to allow us to further analyze at the story level for source categories. For each story, we identified the following metadata from database documentation or through our own analysis: the date of publication and day of the week, headline, duplicate and syndication status, syndication source, author, and source title. Stories include individual articles in newspapers or websites of radio and TV stations, broadcast segments, and blog posts. For a detailed overview of the source and story metadata, see Online Appendix B. For each story, we identified the following metadata from database documentation or through our own analysis: the date of publication and day of the week, headline, duplicate and syndication status, syndication source, author, and source title. Stories include individual articles in newspapers or websites of radio and TV stations, broadcast segments, and blog posts. The first author read each text in the corpus of all non-duplicated stories at least twice, engaging in an inductive process to generate more targeted research questions and themes. The second author also read all stories that database and headline searches identified as candidates for duplication or syndication.

2.3.1 Duplicate Stories

Our search of the indexed news sources showed duplicated stories, which we identify as those stories of the same author, date, and publication and which indicate an error in the uploading of data from the source to the indexing database. Of the original 651 stories, 55 were duplicates. We excluded these duplicates from further analysis in the corpus, resulting in a total of 596 stories analyzed. All of the numbers relating to the corpus analysis exclude the duplicate stories.

2.3.2 Syndication Status

In order to understand the scale of syndication across media outlets, our analysis included identifying whether stories were syndicated from wire reports or other source publications. Across the local newspapers, we see frequent use of *Capitol News Illinois* stories throughout the study period as indicated by the byline information (including author name, affiliation, or email) and story titles. Shaw Media, a privately held regional news media chain, which has seven daily and nineteen weeklies (one of the nineteen weeklies has sixteen editions) for a total of forty-one local newspapers, also accounts for a significant source of content in local newspapers, with the frequent repeat of story titles and byline. The second author manually compared syndicated stories from *Capitol News Illinois* and Shaw Media to quantify the extent of this syndication. In-depth results of this status are reported in Section 5 but we find that 343, or 57.6 percent, of the non-duplicated stories in our corpus are syndicated from other sources, primarily from *Capitol News Illinois* or from Shaw Media.

2.4 Comprehensiveness of Corpus and Analytical Approach

After identifying our corpus and conducting a first-round analysis, we engaged in a form of member-checking about our initial interpretation of the data, consulting with five Illinois-based journalists (local TV, nonprofit digital-first, public radio, newspaper, and the AP State House correspondent) and a top editor at a leading digital-first Republican news site to assess the validity of our search approach, our understanding of the news syndication process, and assess the construction of our corpus relative to their understanding of news archiving.

The GOP-site editor noted problems with Google News indexing right-wing media; to address these potential gaps, we did targeted searches for "Darren Bailey" on the top ten highest trafficked Republican digital-first websites in 2020 (the Righting, n.d.). We also discussed our findings with two Illinois politicians, one currently serving in the state legislature as a Democrat and the other, a retired Republican political strategist.

While we do not claim the search is exhaustive, we believe it to be comprehensive and representative. In order to understand the flows of information and to mimic, to our best effort, all the possible content that a member of the public might encounter about Bailey, a single database search was not enough, even though including platform searches does introduce additional uncertainty into the corpus around indexing limitations. For such an extensive, multi-platform corpus construction, however, databases do not provide enough detail about local broadcast news media, and leaving out this content is problematic for understanding our research questions, especially as audience research finds that local television is among the most relied-upon single source of local news for 31 percent of Americans (Pew Research Center, 2023). This approach to triangulation offers a model that can be repeated for further analysis or to examine other micro-level intersections of media and politics. While unique in specifics to our case study, drawing upon the situated experiences of the research team and combining traditional database searches with targeted and organic search enables a comprehensive, multi-platform, cross-media corpus for a temporally bounded media environment. Our complete data can be found on https://digital.sandiego.edu/commstudies_facpub/18/.

3 The Context and Structure for Illinois' Political and Media Ecosystems

Our first research question is: At the local level, what elements of the political ecosystem set the groundwork for Bailey's rise? We draw on both primary empirical research and secondary source scholarship to articulate the context and structure of the underlying political conditions and media environment that buttressed Bailey's ascent: the first "P" and the first "M" in the PMP model. As a whole, we find that Illinois' deep political and cultural divisions between urban/rural and Democrat/Republican offered a fertile conflict frame for Bailey and the news media alike to exploit. Moreover, declines in Illinois' local news media ecosystem and existing patterns of media ownership offered an infrastructure that served to amplify Bailey across the state and country. These divisions and challenges in Illinois are ones present across the US, and reflect the fractured polity that has enabled the renewal of antidemocratic nationalist populist discourse.

3.1 State Political Structure

The PMP approach considers the importance of the structural level of the political ecosystem, or the institutional structures that shape governance; Illinois' rural–urban political and sociocultural divide contextualizes how a challenge to the governor's COVID-19 policies might seed a media storm. Since 1992, Illinois has been "blue" for the purposes of national elections, although 2002 has widely been regarded as the state's "tipping point" to solidly blue, when Democrats captured a trifecta with majorities in both chambers of the state legislature and the governor's office (Paul Simon Public Policy Institute, 2007). While Republicans controlled redistricting in 2001, in 2010, Democrats were able to gerrymander even more favorable election results (Paul Simon Public Policy Institute, 2007). In 2021, Democrats ignored the recommendations of the nonpartisan Princeton Gerrymandering Project, ones even President Obama had encouraged state leaders to consider (Burnett, 2021), and its current electoral map gets an F grade from this group and is classified as "very noncompetitive."

Structurally, the geographic distribution of the state's population enables the urban, Democratic stronghold of Chicago to set the tone for the state's politics. The vast majority of the state's geographic expanse is rural, but its population is urban – two-thirds of the state's 12.8 million population lives within Chicago and its five surrounding "collar" counties. Of Illinois' 102 counties, 83 are classified as "rural" according to the Rural-Urban Continuum Code (USDA, 2013). The only Republican to win a governor's race after 2002 was Bruce Rauner, elected in 2014 in the wake of incumbent Democrat Governor Rod Blagojevich's corruption conviction. Nonetheless, the political reality inside state politics is more complicated. While in 2018, Governor J. B. Pritzker won the gubernatorial election in a landslide, he only won 16 out of the state's 102 counties; in 2020, President Biden won only 14 of Illinois' counties (McKinney, 2022).

3.2 State Political Culture

PMP also considers the importance of the cultural level of a political ecosystem, or the medium term context, such as political polarization and beliefs and norms of political actors. From this perspective, nonurban areas are collectively referred to in Illinois as "downstate," a signifier for anything not part of the

"Chicagoland" urban population hub, regardless of a county's cartesian geographical location to Chicago (Jaffe, 2017). The bogeyman of empowered, corrupt Democrats has long been a thorn in the sides of the Republican downstate politicians, who blame big city Democrats for tanking the financial health and the political reputation of the state. Illinois' politics also reflect a growing rural/urban political divide, one that is becoming more politically polarized over time. Since 2012, Illinois has become increasingly split by rural–urban divides, both politically and demographically; over this span, the five high-population suburban counties outside Chicago have shifted from purple to reliably Democrat (Center for Illinois Politics, 2020).

While rural counties in Illinois are as a whole generally more prosperous than in surrounding states, they nonetheless suffer from problems common to rural areas, such as population declines, aging populations, and corporate consolidations of independent and regional banks, hospitals, and supermarkets. Generally, rural areas are less well funded for education, older, have lower wages, and have less access to healthcare than their urban counterparts. Illinois has lost population as a state, but the rate of population decline is highest in rural areas (Bessler, 2023). Population declines create additional challenges, in part because population size affects state and federal funding. Public stakeholders worry about declines in civic cohesion in rural Illinois; civic organizations such as the Lions, Kiwanis, and Rotary clubs struggle to recruit members, especially in rural locales (Vorva, 2020).

Illinois has long had a reputation for cronyism and corruption. The Department of Justice began keeping statistics for prosecutions for public corruption in 1976; annual totals have long ranked Illinois among the top three most politically corrupt states, per capita, with Chicago often ranked first for the most corrupt federal judicial district (Simpson et al., 2021). Four of the last ten governors spent time in prison (Schmidt, 2022). Recent high-level corruption cases have included prison time for Democratic Governor Rod Blagojevich (2003–2009), who was indicted for "pay to play" schemes, including putting Obama's Senate seat "on sale," and the 2022 indictment for racketeering of the Speaker of the House, Michael J. Madigan, the longest serving state house speaker in the US (Smith, 2022).

3.3 On the Ground: Political Resentment and Political Power

Although our fieldwork and interviews with community leaders generally were after Bailey's media splash, they provide additional qualitative observations about the cultural dimension of the local political and media news ecology. Jim Nowlan, the retired state politician and political science professor who introduced the first author to many of their fieldwork contacts, observed both in public and one-on-one conversations that the character of Illinois politics had changed and that Republicans in Illinois had become more extreme. After barnstorming with a candidate for the state supreme court in 2020, Nolwan observed, "The business Republican party has been overwhelmed by Trumpism." He shared this observation in a number of settings – a different private dinner, a Kiwanis club speech, and with the first author: "A million years ago, you'd go to [campaign and host] an ice cream social and men in white shirts in ties, and they were the hardware store owners, the bankers, the lawyers ... " and now, he noticed "tattoos and rolled up shirts," perhaps hinting to a shift in these communities. "My theory is that these folks all wish they tried a little harder but need a place to take out anger."

At a small private dinner hosted by Nowlan in the run-up to the 2022 gubernatorial primary that Bailey ultimately won, local politicians observed growing support for Trumpian Republicanism but still saw Bailey's brand of politics as anathema to the state political culture. A county party leader said that in 2020 he had 400 Trump signs to give out, but he couldn't get anyone to take a sign during an in-person party meeting. When he posted on Facebook that he'd be in the town square handing signs out, his "phone blew up." In some cases, people didn't want to admit to taking the signs for themselves, and he recalled how one man who took a sign said, "That's my wife, not me." When the first author suggested that Bailey might win the Republican gubernatorial primary, a longtime politician responded, "The candidate for Republican governor is not in the race yet," and another politician proclaimed, "What's Bailey got to run on? COVID is almost over," failing to foresee the full extent of Bailey's illiberal politics.

Fieldwork also revealed just how community leaders of struggling small towns and prominent farmers saw themselves as abandoned by state political power. Just after the 2022 gubernatorial primary season began, the first author had breakfast with a Champaign County farmer and a board member of Champaign County Farm Bureau at the local pancake house infamous to some locals for violating COVID protocols. Both detailed shifts in the state's political culture. The farmer, a self-identified moderate Republican, noted "It was so scary on Jan 6, people are not picking up how scary it got" and spoke to the downstream effects of the political extremism in the state, maligning "the middle has disappeared." The farm bureau leader expressed the extent of continued disempowerment for Republicans in Illinois. He noted, "State and local [politics] – [they are] controlled by Chicago, and it's never going to change. They have two-thirds of the population between Cook County and the collar, they're not going to see a decrease in that, they have control." The resignation expressed about the local political culture and sentiment among civically and politically involved downstate community members helps situate how local rural political culture might be primed to boost up one of their own – and be open to supporting a local candidate who reflected their sense of disempowerment by standing up to the Democratic machine.

3.4 Media: Structural and Cultural Contexts

A closer look at the structural and cultural elements of the Illinois media ecology helps provide additional context for understanding how a politician like Bailey might benefit from its preexisting vulnerabilities. As discussed in Usher (2022), as of 2002, Illinois was home to approximately 546 newspapers, including metro dailies and community weeklies, though in 2021 this dropped to about 460 newspapers. All but four of Illinois' 102 counties are served by some form of local newspaper, usually a weekly, although the News Deserts research project points out that by their estimates, thirty-three counties only have a single source of news (Abernathy, 2020), although some of these counties have small, centrally located populations that may still be relatively well served by local news efforts. In 2021, state lawmakers were so concerned about the decline of local news in the state that they created a blue ribbon commission, the Illinois Local Journalism Task Force. The report, released in 2024, provides a comprehensive overview of the challenges facing Illinois citizens' ability to have access to reliable, verified, and up-to-date local news during the period under study. As per this report, journalism jobs in Illinois have declined by 86 percent since 2005, and the state (and region's) most prominent newspaper, the *Chicago Tribune*, roughly mirrored these losses, losing 82 percent of its staff since 2006 leading to its retrenchment from statewide and regional coverage.

Nonetheless, Illinois is home to a vibrant constellation of nonprofit and digital-first news outlets. Illinois was the nonprofit ProPublica's first state-focused effort in 2017. Chicago's local digital news experiments include City Bureau, known for its Documentors project, which trains local residents to cover public meetings, and Block Club Chicago, which provides hyperlocal coverage of the city's neighborhoods. While the *Chicago Tribune* has suffered, the *Chicago Sun-Times* remains a bright hope for those worried about the declines in local news: it is now a nonprofit that is owned and operated in partnership with Chicago's public radio station, WBEZ. However, local news task force notes that fewer and fewer state dollars are going directly to public media – from $4,011,976 in 2009 to $1,657,800 in 2024 – and the report notes that public media funding per capita in Illinois is roughly 12 cents, the lowest of its Midwestern neighbor states.

Notably, sharp declines in State House coverage have been addressed via a nonprofit syndicated news service, *Capitol News Illinois*. Founded by the Illinois Press Association in 2019 as a nonprofit news service as a response to diminished State House coverage, it is backed by the Robert R. McCormick Foundation and the Illinois Broadcasters Foundation. According to the Illinois Press Association (IPA), its 460 newspaper members and 100 broadcasters receive daily coverage; *Capitol News Illinois* has also pursued content and reporting partnerships with the for-profit Lee Enterprises newspapers and with ProPublica (IPA, n.d.)

Still, downstate news ecologies face growing structural challenges. Newspapers like the *Peoria Journal Star*, the *Southern Illinoisan* (Carbondale), the *Pantagraph* (Bloomington), and the *News-Gazette* (Champaign), which serve smaller cities, have also been challenged by an assortment of issues. These include population loss (thus a decline in subscriptions) to declines in locally owned businesses that were long counted upon for advertising. The high distribution costs of print and mail delivery have long plagued newspapers but hit newspapers with rural readers harder – there's simply more gas (and more distance) required to reach the same number of readers compared to urban news outlets. COVID-19 accelerated challenges to rural newspapers in Illinois; on March 31, 2020, Illinois' 22nd Century Media, publisher of fourteen suburban and exurban Illinois publications, closed, blaming "the economic impact of the coronavirus on all small businesses, from which we earn a large majority of our advertising" (Usher, 2022). While local radio broadcasts are often able to take advantage of uncrowded, locally owned spectrum, these stations largely feature religious talk or country music. Friedland et al. (2022) have observed that these local radio stations rarely offer much local news aside from daily announcements. As per Usher (2023), local television news is more a genre than a descriptor in these areas; St. Louis channels reach into southwest Illinois, while northwest Illinois stations also cover neighboring Iowa; rural dwellers in southeastern Illinois get their local television news from stations based in Indiana and Kentucky. In interviews, one public official explained that her town was covered by St. Louis news with some frequency because one of the lead reporters had grown up in the area – but for that, she wouldn't expect to see much about rural Illinois on local television.

There is also a downstate digital local news hole: outside of Chicago and its five surrounding counties, only 12 percent of the state has access to daily, geographically specific newspaper journalism, while 89 percent of these newspapers are weekly, as per Usher (2022). More than one-fifth of rural newspapers are not available on the web: Twenty-two percent of newspapers outside the Chicagoland region do not have a website, while 40 percent have a Facebook page, meaning that rural users looking for the digital versions of local news are more likely to find it on Facebook than on the open web (Usher, 2023). Given this legacy information environment, Illinois rural dwellers likely turn primarily to social and digital media for access to news and information – and more likely than not, Facebook, given that two-thirds of rural residents say they use it (Auxier & Anderson 2021). Rural dwellers tend to rely more on digital social networks to learn about events and issues of local civic importance (Nah et al., 2021). However, local news on Facebook has received low engagement (Weber, Andringa & Napoli, 2019), suggesting that the rural residents looking at Facebook for news and information about their communities and beyond may not be even interacting with local news sources. Generally, the diminished local news ecology's structural challenges have cultural import, with key informants across the state worrying that the lack of local news has undermined both the efficacy of nonpartisan political information and has been replaced by hyper-partisan conspiracy content. Knowing more about the cultural context of the local news ecology helps situate both how Bailey was covered as well as how rural audiences consumed news and information about COVID-19 and about politics, more generally.

3.5 On the Ground: Local News Ecology, Culture, Local News Holes, and Local Politics

Local stakeholders worried about the loss of professionally produced local news and its implications for civic life in Illinois. Community leaders worried that the diminished local footprint would cause community members to turn to partisan news sources for their information. At a dinner at the Peoria Country Club, the former editorial and opinion editor of the *Peoria Journal Star* pointed out that Peoria now had 3.5 reporters covering a metropolitan region of 370,000 people. "It's impossible, people want a lot, we can't do it," she noted, and mourned the loss of the newspaper's role in helping the community the community advocate for changes to the city "We did editorial crusades that actually helped Peoria," she added, explaining how the newspaper had helped avoid cuts to funding for the public bus system, redevelop downtown Peoria to include a riverfront museum, and develop the local rails-to-trails infrastructure. She also noted the diminished attention afforded to local-level candidates, pointing to the decline of local endorsements.

> "We used to talk to people running for office . . . we would even interview judicial candidates. Now it's hard to look up and learn who is running for office . . . People might know who is running for Congress, but not their judges."

But simply having a newspaper did not guarantee the kind of robust coverage that some of these civic leaders might want. For instance, the Peoria dinner included a local businessman from a small town who owned the hunting and fishing gear shop, was on the city council, and also owned the local newspaper. "When we write about city council, I take my byline off it," he said, and shared with the group a recent controversy over residential chicken coop laws. When the first author looked at the newspaper, the husband-and-wife team that owned it had bylined almost every article of any substance. Even in places that still had community news, the geographic and social connections between newspaper owners and town residents did not quite permit the same kind of independent, dispassionate journalism that is imagined by scholars writing about press and politics in the US.

Others theorized that the lack of locally specific news might be leading to more expensive elections and put more pressure on relying on party-provided communications. Former US Congress Rep. and US Department of Transportation Secretary Ray LaHood pointed out the differences he saw in local campaigns given the diminished coverage, "Candidates are not selling [themselves] through, editorial pages, but political [parties]. To win an election you have to buy it. They sell [ads] on TV, they use money to put out mailers." Another local civic leader from a different county noted, "We have three candidates for city council, the only way you'd know is signs in the front yard." The civic leader, who owned a bike shop in a rural town, pointed out how "we have the end of local editorials, the end of local political reporters, it's a huge change ... you send enough of them and they begin to believe the ad and mailers." These mailers, party-financed, might be providing more information about who was actually running in any one place, and any attack ads would escape scrutiny from the local press. At the redistricting dinner, a recently elected circuit court judge was praised for winning a campaign that otherwise no one in the county had information about. Nowlan complimented the new judge, noting, "We talked about social ... he was knocking on the doors everywhere, no one knows who is running for judge [most of the time], but his name was everywhere: on the radio, on signs," pointing to the need to go beyond local newspapers to find other ways to break through the local political information vacuum. This worried civic leaders the first author spoke with at both dinners/focus groups, in part because Illinois has so many elected units of government and the vast majority received little coverage from any outlet.

Community leaders worried about the lack of locally specific political news and information, concerned that the diminished local footprint left rural residents vulnerable to misinformation. Public health officials also provided qualitative support for the tendency of local politicians to take their talking points from partisan news and national party elites. As one official explained the resistance in her community to COVID mitigation, "I truly believe this was stoked... federally, by the person in the presidency stoked by Fox News, but we had a local element that played on that." Another public health official described how she had signed up for every Republican website she could find to get ahead of the misinformation percolating in local conservative circles. These insights from public health officials are instructive, as they point to the lived experience of how national politics and media coverage intersected with the local political culture and the news and information circulating in any one community. As the pandemic went on, many local business leaders and elected officials would resist efforts to mitigate the pandemic; however, Bailey was the first to challenge the governor and was the beneficiary of "media storm" coverage.

3.6 Political and News Ecologies: Structure and Culture

Taken together, this overview of the structural and cultural elements of the political ecology and media ecology of Illinois helps situate Bailey's breakthrough. On one hand, the downstate political culture reflects a long-standing frustration with the dominance of Chicago and its surrounding areas in state government. Generally, downstate leaders view any sort of change in this structure as somewhat impossible, but the continued disempowerment of downstate has bred a quiet resentment seen elsewhere where there are rural–urban political and cultural divides (Cramer, 2016; Friedland et al., 2022). Even after his national breakthrough, Republican politicians underestimated just how much Bailey would shift the direction of the Republican party. While temporally our qualitative data was gathered after the media storm that enveloped Bailey, these perspectives do help explain the space in Illinois politics for someone willing to directly challenge Pritzker. However, Bailey's lawsuit against the governor was more than just politics as usual, it was an attack on the legitimacy of the democratically elected governor's power.

The overarching political culture and structure might have been receptive to extremist politics. However, the impact of shifts in the news ecology is less clear. Given the relatively diminished role of local news and the paucity of local political coverage, just how would a local politician gain traction? Local politicians were not being covered by local newspapers in any depth, leaving party communications via Facebook and mailers and yard signs as the primary source of local political information. Local television was anything but local, having a reach and coverage mandate far beyond the happenings of any one town. For any politician to be able to get themselves on local television beaming across not just Illinois but adjacent states, it would be a win. The odds against a low-level politician ever being noticed by national news media seems thin – making the question as to just how Bailey became enveloped in this massive sweep of local to national coverage all the more compelling for research. The following sections probe the politician's rise from obscurity to Fox News in a week – as well as how his actions and this coverage influenced copycat politicians.

4 The Rise of Darren Bailey: PMP and the Political Economy of the News Industry

These structural and cultural aspects of the political and media ecology are also augmented by the more immediate or "situational" level of the political and media ecosystems during the COVID-19 pandemic, the short-term circumstances that immediately impact political activity. With the pandemic hopefully in the background, it is also helpful to remember the fraught period when COVID was a new, deadly virus without a vaccine and when there was still limited knowledge about effective treatment for patients. In the immediate onset of the pandemic, cities took the brunt of the deaths and intensity of the pandemic, although rural counties quickly caught up with their own poor COVID-19 health outcomes, eventually surpassing rural areas in COVID deaths and hospitalizations (Callaghan et al., 2021).

In this section, we offer a descriptive answer to "How did coverage unfold?" Drawing from our corpus, we consider the aggregate patterns in the news coverage and draw attention to key events and pivotal media coverage between April 23, 2020, and May 2, 2020, we see as the most significant factors in establishing Bailey's prominence, inspiring copycat actions, and as influential in driving the coverage forward. The PMP model suggests that there is a "situational" context – literally, temporally, something happens. In this case, the storyline is set in motion by Pritzker's announcement on April 23, 2020, instituting a new stay-at-home order effective until May 30, 2020. The political dynamic evolved throughout the week, providing a new series of events and actors to cover. Bailey was the first mover, and his lawsuit is referenced in most stories as the rationale/background for the newest challenge. He became the figurehead for the Republican resistance against the COVID-19 precautions in deep blue Illinois, anointed by local, regional, national, and Republican news media. By the end of our ten-day period, Bailey's initial challenge was followed by lawsuits from two different local politicians and an Illinois church, along with mentions in local and national news media of at least eight low-level elected officials across Illinois who promised not to enforce Pritzker's safer at home order. Our approach considers:

1. How coverage evolved over time: Across medium, outlet, and as part of the PMP dynamic
2. How links across and between news outlets impact and amplify Bailey's public presence

We discuss possible interpretations for why these particular moments, specific stories, and attention from specific outlets might have facilitated Bailey's rise due to the structure of the news industry. A more detailed timeline can be found in Online Appendix A. After tracking the aggregate trends, we apply a political economy analysis. This approach considers how factors like ownership, syndication/content-sharing partnerships, institutional isomorphism, and partisan ideology influence news coverage. This enables us to begin answering the second research question: how the practices and challenges facing the news industry – local, regional, national, and partisan media – might serve to amplify extremists. This analysis sheds insight into whether the structure of the news industry itself set Bailey up for his rapid ascent.

Overall, our corpus challenges some long-standing assumptions about the role of local news in informing communities. Our findings also highlight the importance of content diversity, not just source diversity: while there are 126 different sources in our corpus, which includes newspaper, digital-first, radio, broadcast, wire, and cable news outlets, the actual *content diversity* is minuscule. Before we began corpus analysis, we did not know just how Bailey was able to burst onto the national scene. We were surprised to see that the AP – and therefore national news coverage – was present from day one. Bailey also benefited from local television news coverage carrying his Facebook Live announcement of the lawsuit – also on day one. As we expected, there was indeed far more local and regional coverage than national and international coverage (543 stories or 91.1 percent percent compared to 53 stories or 8.9 percent). We also expected newspapers to make up the bulk of our corpus (78.5 percent or 468 stories; of these, local and regional newspaper stories account for 91.9 percent and 3.6 percent of all stories). However, we were also surprised to see so much redundancy in our corpus such that three headlines, with minor variations, alone account for 111 stories in our corpus (18.6 per cent). We discuss these findings in greater detail in the sections that follow.

4.1 Aggregate Trends and Major Moments in Coverage

If Bailey's rise is a media storm, "when news outlets become suddenly and strongly riveted to a storyline," resulting in a period of "sudden, high, and sustained media attention to an event or issue" (Boydstun, Hardy & Walgrave 2014, p. 509), we would expect to see a Gaussian distribution over our stories. This is different from the punctuated equilibrium that we would see with more routine coverage – flashes of coverage and then nothing. Boydstun et al. (2014) propose explosiveness, amount, and duration as key criteria for identifying a storm, and have identified empirical benchmarks for each. The surge of attention to a specific topic must be 150 percent more or 2.5 times compared to the previous week, the volume of coverage itself captures at least 20 percent of the total front page, and (c) lasts for an entire week of coverage, which the authors point to as a "significant period" at least in terms of journalism's focus on any one particular issue or subject (Walgrave, 2017, p. 556). As our research proceeds somewhat differently because of the case approach, these empirical guideposts are only rough anchors for interpreting the patterns we see in the coverage.

Given the current state of the American news industry and trends in audience attention, Bailey's breakthrough and the amplification of his public profile would seem to be fighting against the odds. Still, it seems unlikely that he would be able to capture national media attention so quickly and effectively as an "unknown." Was Bailey just in the right place at the right time with the right antics? Perhaps. A previous Bailey stunt, a legislative caucus to kick Chicago out of Illinois, was received with little notice outside the inside-Springfield/State House crowd. Certainly some element of the overall context for newsworthiness given the mix of events in the world – serendipity or chance – seems to be at work, as media storm scholars have suggested (Boydstun et al., 2014). We expected that a small-time, first-term, state house representative announcing a lawsuit in a small county courthouse would be unlikely to generate national media attention from the start. Generally, preexisting literature posits local news is more geographically proximate and that "knowns" within a smaller community might not merit any attention for news outlets targeted at bigger, national audiences (Usher, 2021). Moreover, local news outlets have widely been theorized as playing an important surveillance role in communities; in practice, local and regional journalists complain that their work is siphoned up by national news outlets without adequate credit (Hester & Gibson, 2007; Usher 2018).

Yet Bailey was able to generate this coverage – in part because of links between news outlets that facilitate the rapid distribution of identical content/ news coverage across partner organizations. Despite the challenges facing the news industry, the structure of the American news industry remains interlinked through ownership, syndication/content-sharing partnerships, institutional isomorphism, and partisan ideology – and as a result, the potential for a politician to win big like Bailey is latent within the system itself. We refer to this content sharing as syndication, although that term has a more specific connotation in the news industry that usually refers to licensing content from another news organization, most often a wire service like the AP. We use syndication as shorthand for chain ownership/shared corporate ownership that facilitates the distribution of identical stories to its news outlets – including local television and newspapers. Similarly, the network membership model of public media enables member stations to repurpose identical content drawn from other public media outlets, although content-sharing agreements may be specific to individual stations.

4.2 Story Count by Medium

Looking across the type of news outlet – newspaper, digital-first, radio, local television, and national television, we were curious how the type of medium itself might be connected to the overall distribution in our coverage (see Figure 2). Notably, the most coverage comes from newspapers – 78.5 percent or 468 stories in the corpus are drawn from newspapers. As noted earlier, newspapers are often considered to be the "keystone" media of local communities, providing the most original coverage about any one place (Nielsen, 2015).

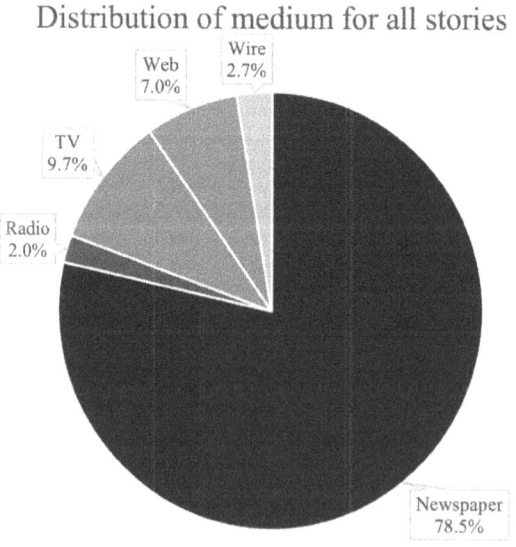

Figure 2 Distribution of medium for all stories.

Both digital-first and television news account for roughly even proportions of coverage in our corpus. The digital-first content also includes sixteen stories from right-wing outlets (both regional and national outlets) that have a digital reach that transcends geography and audiences in the tens of millions (*Gateway Pundit* alone has 68 million unique visitors a month) (Chen et al., 2022). Local television remains a key source of news and information for about 31 percent of people, according to Pew (2023), suggesting that the few stories about Bailey that did play on local television likely extended his name to a wider group of Illinois residents who most likely lived far outside his home district.

We find some variation in the peak of coverage for the medium of publications in our corpus. On April 29, the most stories overall were published (158) as well as the most newspaper stories (135). Radio (4), wire (5), and TV (18) coverage all peaked a day earlier on Tuesday, April 28, while web-based coverage reached a peak of 9 stories on both Monday, April 27, and Wednesday, April 29 (see Figure 3).

4.3 Story Count and Key Events

We then separated our corpus into national, international, regional (having a statewide or Midwestern regional audience), and local (targeting a defined, specific geographical market). We then combined the national and international categories into one group (this included national GOP media outlets) and both local and regional coverage, as a combined category of a more general "local" coverage designation to assess aggregate "local versus national" coverage. As a whole, there was far more local and regional coverage (543 stories) than national or international coverage (53 stories); Bailey's national coverage was in high-impact cable, newspaper, and digital-first outlets, while the bulk of Bailey's local and regional coverage came from newspapers (see Figure 4).

The jumping off for the case study is April 23, a Thursday, when Bailey filed his lawsuit, with ten stories (two national, ten local). The AP covered the story from the get-go; an AP State House bureau staffer explained retrospectively that the lawsuit was newsworthy because "a sitting legislator filed what they saw as a legitimate lawsuit challenging the governor's powers during this critical moment" of the unfolding pandemic. The AP story, then, is a critical jump-start for Bailey, as it not only legitimizes interest in the story, but it also gives it an immediate national profile (see Figure 5 for a breakdown of the geography of stories by day).

On April 24, there were some scattered early stories about Bailey and the lawsuit (ten national, one local); notably, Bailey also created an additional opportunity for further engagement with the press, offering his own press conference the same day to further publicize his lawsuit. Journalists also asked Pritzker

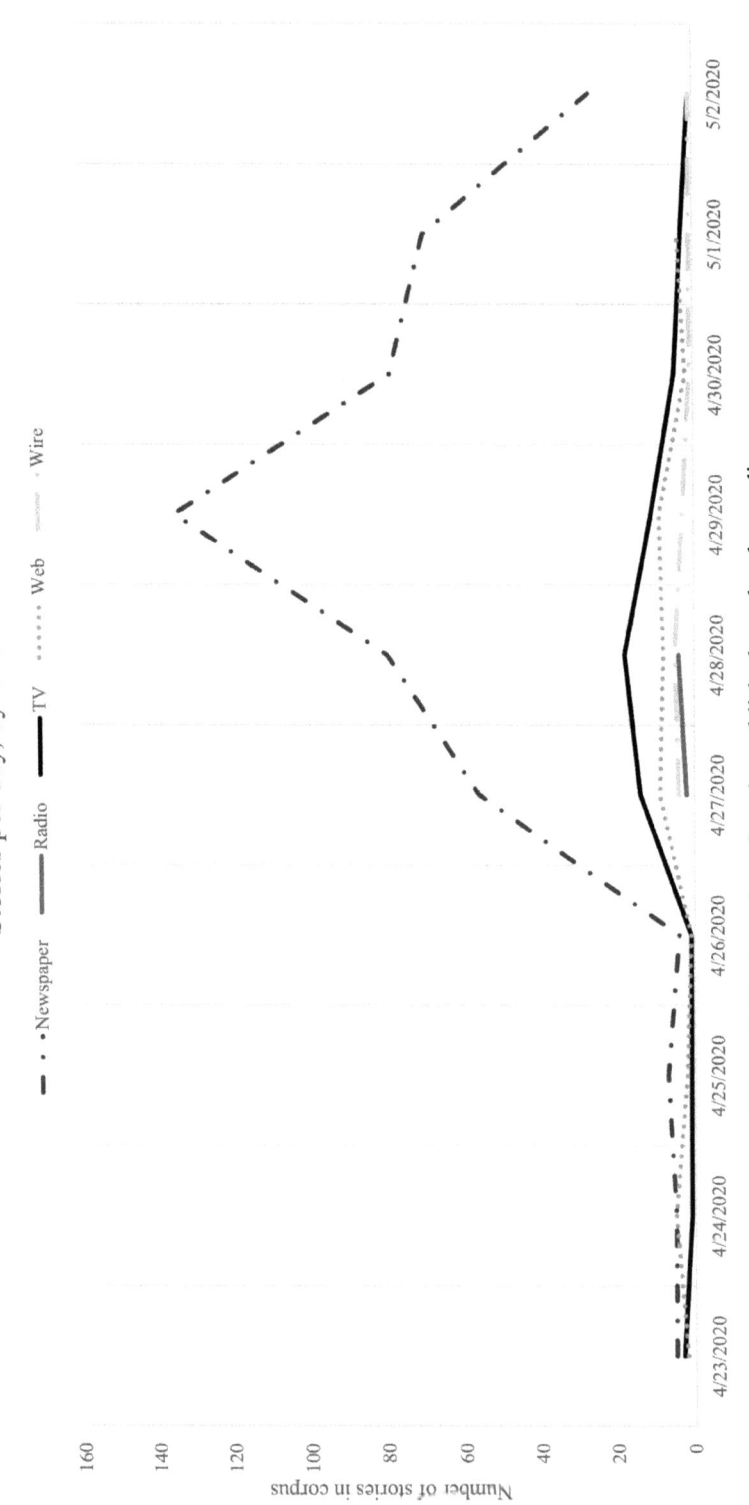

Figure 3 Total number of stories published per day, by medium.

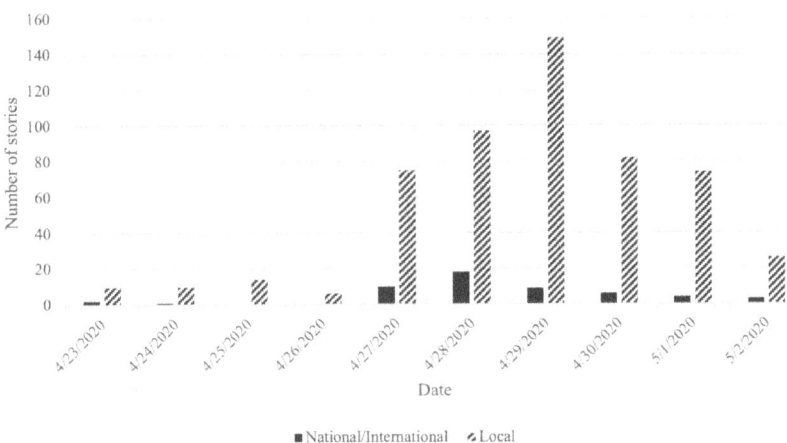

Figure 4 Comparison chart of national/international and local coverage by day.

for comment on the lawsuit, both legitimizing Bailey's lawsuit and drawing Pritzker himself into the conflict. Notably, the AP coverage on April 23 preceded coverage by the nonprofit state house journalism outlet, *Capitol News Illinois*, whose broad mandate is to report on events from the Capitol for news outlets across the state who otherwise would not have their own state house reporter.

On April 25 (fourteen local) and April 26 (six local), the weekend, the "P" or the politicians do not actually have any further response. Still, Pritzker's response to Bailey from the 24th fuels most of the weekend's coverage of activity in the Illinois State House. The insider *CapitolFax* State House blog accuses Bailey of causing the conflict for personal gain and attention, which may have also helped direct additional reporting attention by other outlets to the emerging conflict.

On Monday, April 27, the a Bailey-friendly Republican judge issues his ruling against Pritzker. The coverage begins to spike (eighty-five stories, compared to forty-three for the first four days), a 50.6 percent jump, meeting the general threshold for "explosive" coverage (seventy-five local, ten national). The ruling came just five days and two business days after the initial lawsuit. While we can't know the answer to the counterfactual – in this case, a longer time between the lawsuit and decision – we suspect that the close timing between the lawsuit and the ruling likely sustained media attention on the case. With a decision in place, there is a discrete news event/time peg that jump-starts more sustained attention from these outlets.

We surmise that the flood of coverage on April 27 also emerged in part because of the ruling that legitimated the merits of the lawsuit itself, with Pritzker's supposed overreach checked by an Illinois court. The lawsuit may have been an

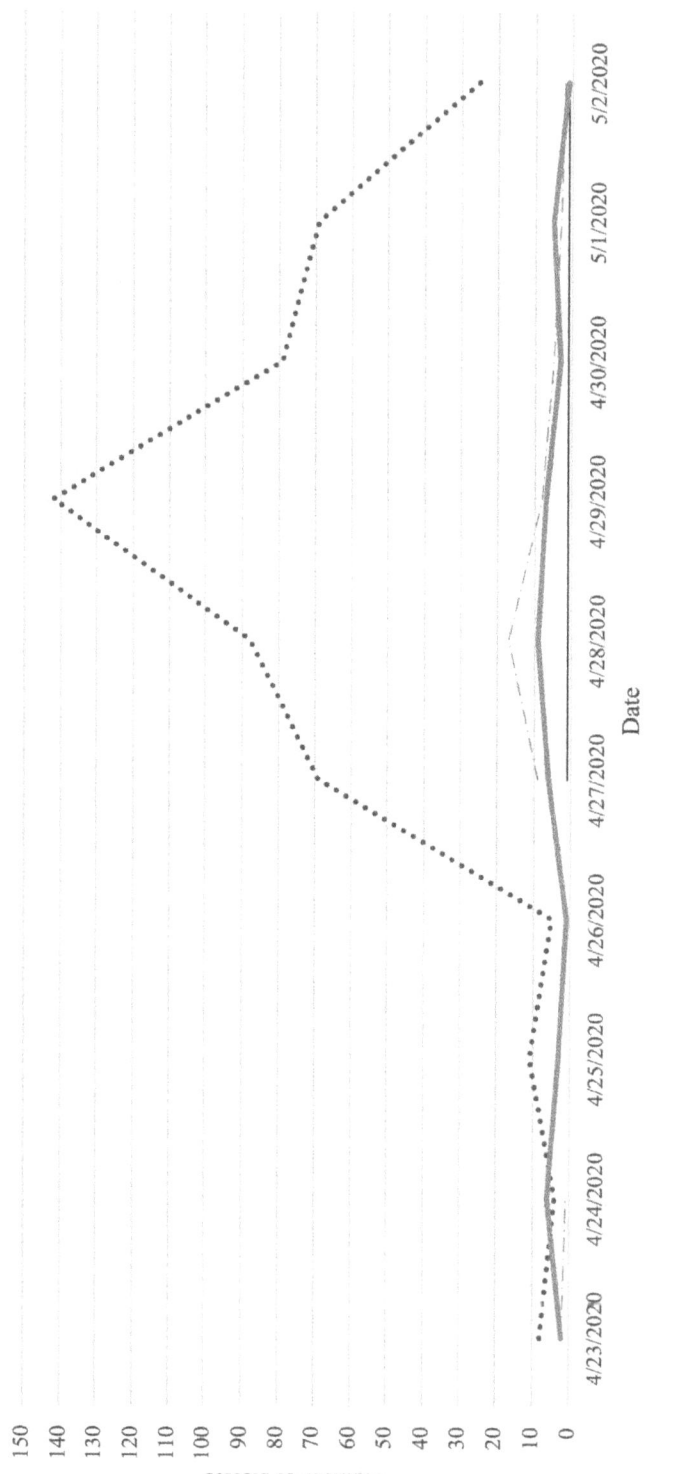

Figure 5 Geographic coverage of stories by day.

attention grab, but now there were actual legal implications; the ruling's strong language gave additional power to Bailey's contention that Pritzker was undermining civil liberties in the US Simply filing a lawsuit against a governor might not draw the attention of large national outlets beyond the AP State House bureau. The unusual ruling, which applied only to Bailey, also provided an element of novelty to the unfolding story, which we discuss further in Section 5.

On April 28, the Illinois Attorney General filed notice of an appeal against Bailey Along with rumblings of a second suit to be filed by the head of the Trump campaign in Illinois (John Cabello), other local politicians garnered press attention for announcing their refusal to comply with Pritzker's executive order. This is the peak of national coverage (ninety-seven local, seventeen national); one day *before* local coverage peaks. There are two possible reasons for this; national coverage could drive more local coverage. Or the confluence of coverage of stories from the lawsuit verdict issued the day prior, April 27, occurred on April 28, the day after the lawsuit, while local media had more reason to remain engaged in the follow-up conflict between Pritzker and Bailey, especially after new local politicians come forward to denounce Pritzker's order.

On April 29 (149 local, 9 national), Bailey makes his appearance on Fox News' *The Ingraham Angle*. This is also when coverage overall peaks (158 stories). While the Republican media ecosystem is also present from the start, it is notable that digital pickup from *Gateway Pundit* and *Breitbart* precede Bailey's appearance on Ingraham on April 29. On April 30 (eighty-two local, six national), Bailey garnered an institutional Republican media capstone: the right-leaning opinion page of the *WSJ* featuring a contribution that heralds Bailey's bravery. For a small town politician, an appearance on Ingraham and even just a mention in the *WSJ* is tantamount to a small coronation: these appearances cement Bailey's standing as a crusader against Pritzker.

While we did choose to limit the coverage to a ten-day period, after the peak on April 29 (158 total stories), the coverage increasingly became less about Bailey and more about his role as the instigator of the resistance that followed. In short, after May 1 (seventy-eight total stories), his initial splash had broken the surface, and he was part of the conversation, not just the object of storm-style media coverage (see Figure 6). The most intense coverage was over a five-day period, but the lawsuit is a subject of media attention for all of the ten days under study.

4.4 The Political Economy of the News Industry

In this section, we apply a political economy approach – an inductive analysis that considers how factors like ownership, syndication/content-sharing partnerships, institutional isomorphism, and partisan ideology influence news coverage. This

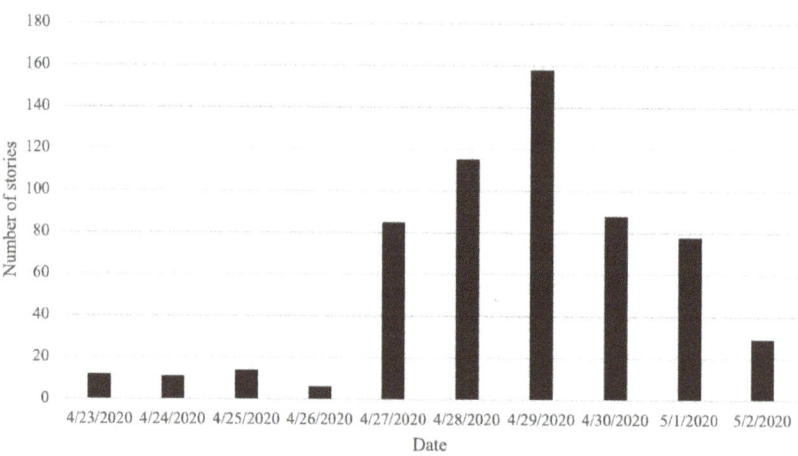

Figure 6 Total stories published by day.

analysis sheds insight into whether the structure of the news industry itself set Bailey up for his rapid ascent. A closer look at the content itself supports that while newspaper stories made up the bulk of the coverage of Bailey's lawsuit, these sources did not actually provide unique content for each geographically relevant community. Overall, while there are 126 different sources in our corpus that include newspaper, digital-first, radio, broadcast, wire, and cable news outlets, the actual *content diversity* is miniscule.

Syndicated coverage and content sharing played a critical role in spreading news of the lawsuit beyond its immediate geography in tiny Clay County. Via the AP, and its network of 1400 newspapers in the US – the story immediately had a national and potentially international footprint. So Bailey's breakthrough on April 23 did not have to percolate in local news before reaching national news audiences. Notably, right-wing news outlets ran these AP stories, with few changes: on day 1, April 23, the *Washington Times* ran the AP story. This fact-based AP story boosted Bailey to the attention of right-wing partisans, just by recycling the same story for a right-wing audience. *Reuters* covered the lawsuit on April 27, giving the event another national and international boost. Of the seven weekdays in our sample, there is only one day where our corpus does not include an AP or Reuters news story. The sixteen wire stories we captured in our corpus are the ones we found within our specific search parameters, but these stories were available to Reuters and AP customers across the world. The AP was just one of many outlets in the corpus that connected across a wider distribution network to other news outlets – both in terms of the number of outlets and geographic reach, either through content partnerships such as syndication or wire coverage or via shared ownership.

On April 30, 2020, Bailey's lawsuit was aggregated in a *USA Today* roundup of newsworthy events happening across all fifty states, providing additional burst to his coverage. *USA Today*, the flagship Gannett Newspaper, created a news hub to surface and share content with other Gannett newspapers; Gannett owns news outlets in 220 news markets across 43 states and estimates a total weekly *print* readership of 2.9 million; while just a brief, the Bailey story received considerable amplification thanks to this network (Gannett fact sheet, 2024).

Regional newspaper coverage (statewide outlets) from both *Capitol News Illinois* and *Chicago Tribune* began reporting on the story on April 24, a day after local television stations, Bailey's local newspaper, and the AP covered the story. The *Chicago Tribune*, which still holds a reputation for the most well-regarded newspaper in the Midwest, along with the AP coverage may have drawn further national attention to the case. Local news consolidation also played an amplifying role in boosting Bailey's name across the state through newspapers, television, and radio. Even at the headline level, news organizations offer highly redundant coverage. Across our 596 different news stories in our corpus, we find evidence of duplicative headlines that also, on their own, serve to reinforce dominant frame constructions and amplify, quite literally, the people in the news via their appearance in headlines. While some sources tweaked story headlines, we used the byline and cross-check of the story content to identify the limited range of original content making up the overall media conversation about Bailey during the study period. Stories syndicated from *Capitol News Illinois* and by Shaw Media account for 303 total stories, or 50.8 percent of the stories in our corpus overall.

The graphs that follow show both the percentage of syndicated stories by date and the total number of syndicated stories across the unfolding story. Notably, between April 27 and April 30, the period with the most coverage across our corpus, more than 40 percent of stories *every day* were syndicated in some way; on the day with the most stories, April 29, 115 out of the 158 total stories from that day were syndicated (69 percent) – meaning that there was considerable content duplication (see Figure 7 for the percentage of stories syndicated by date and Figure 8 for the total stories syndicated by date).

Most scholarly and popular press literature about the cutbacks in local news suggests that there is less political reporting, not more, especially about state politics. Thus, we might expect the role local newspapers played in amplifying Bailey's name recognition across the state to be minimal – although the overall corpus is almost 80 percent composed of newspaper coverage (local, regional, national, and international). Of the total local news coverage (combining local and regional into one category) 338 of the 543 local stories (62 percent), were

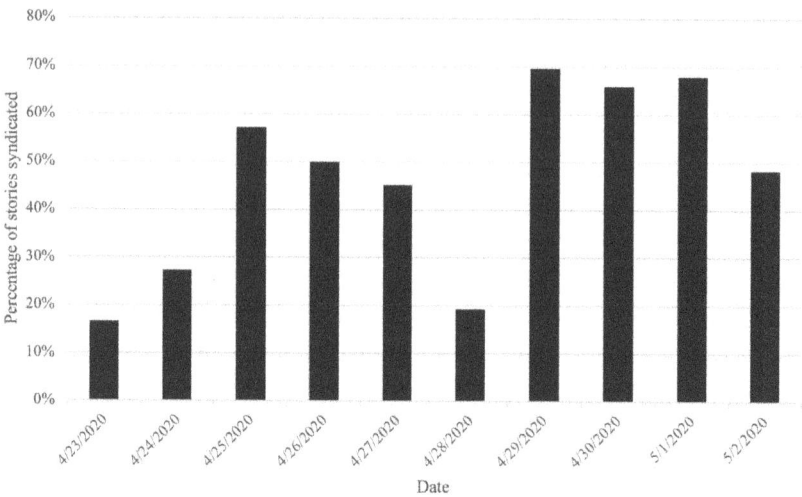

Figure 7 Percentage of stories syndicated by day.

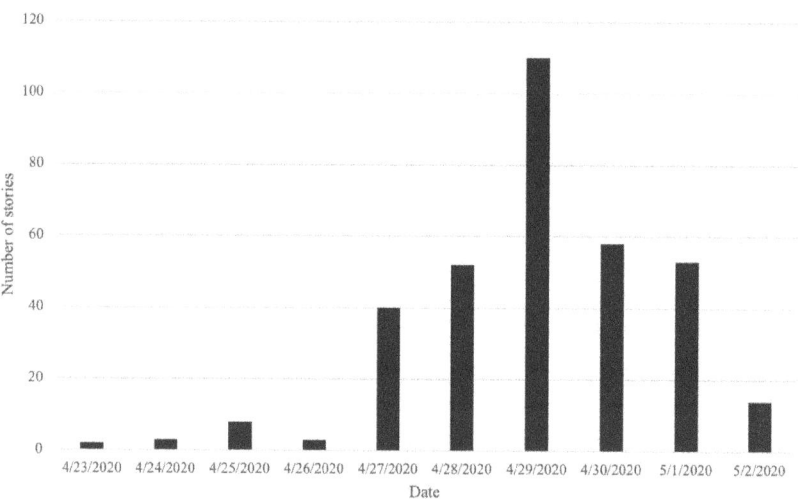

Figure 8 Total number of syndicated stories by day.

syndicated from elsewhere – in other words, these were not originally bylined stories by the outlet itself. The bulk of this coverage came from *Capitol News Illinois* and Shaw Media. Some of this syndication was ironically in response to shortages of news coverage. Recall *Capital News Illinois*, founded by the Illinois Press Association in 2019 as a nonprofit news service, was developed to support quality state house coverage available across the state, with its 460 newspapers and 100 broadcasters receiving daily coverage. This means that *Capitol News Illinois* has significant reach across the state, but each outlet has access to the same set of identical stories: amplification without content diversity.

Figure 9 shows the number of stories written by *Capitol News Illinois* staff writers (193 total) and the frequency with which those stories are repeated across the corpus, in 60 different sources. Across our entire corpus, *Capitol News Illinois* stories accounted for 32.7 percent of the total corpus and 39 percent of all local news stories in our corpus based on our comparison of titles and authors across the data set.

Three headlines, with minor variations, alone account for 107 stories in our corpus (18 percent): April 29 – "Illinois ramps up testing, staffing at long-term care facilities"; April 30 – "AG asks Supreme Court to weigh in on Bailey's lawsuit" (note, this is Illinois' state Supreme Court); and May 1 – "Bailey, attorney say new info a 'game changer' in case against stay-at-home order." Table 1 shows a list of headlines of syndicated stories from *Capitol News Illinois*.

In addition, our corpus also contains syndicated coverage from Shaw Media, a privately held media chain in Illinois, which owns thirty-eight newspapers and nine radio stations in Illinois and estimates a monthly reach of 2.5 million

Table 1 Syndicated stories from *Capitol News Illinois*

Date	Syndicated story	Story count
April 24	Lawmaker sues Pritzker, alleges improper use of emergency powers	17
April 26	State reaches COVID-19 testing goal for third straight day as cases rise	9
April 27	Pritzker blasts GOP rep's lawsuit, says 2 downstate counties have highest death rates	13
April 28	Pritzker blasts lawmaker exempted from stay-at-home order by court	7
April 28	AG to appeal judge's ruling halting stay-at-home order against lawmaker	7
April 29	Second state lawmaker files suit against Pritzker stay-at-home order	18
April 29	Republicans call for reopening legislative session	10
April 29	Illinois ramps up testing, staffing at long-term care facilities	30
April 30	AG asks Supreme Court to weigh in on Bailey's lawsuit	40
May 1	Bailey, attorney say new info a 'game changer' in case against stay-at-home order	37

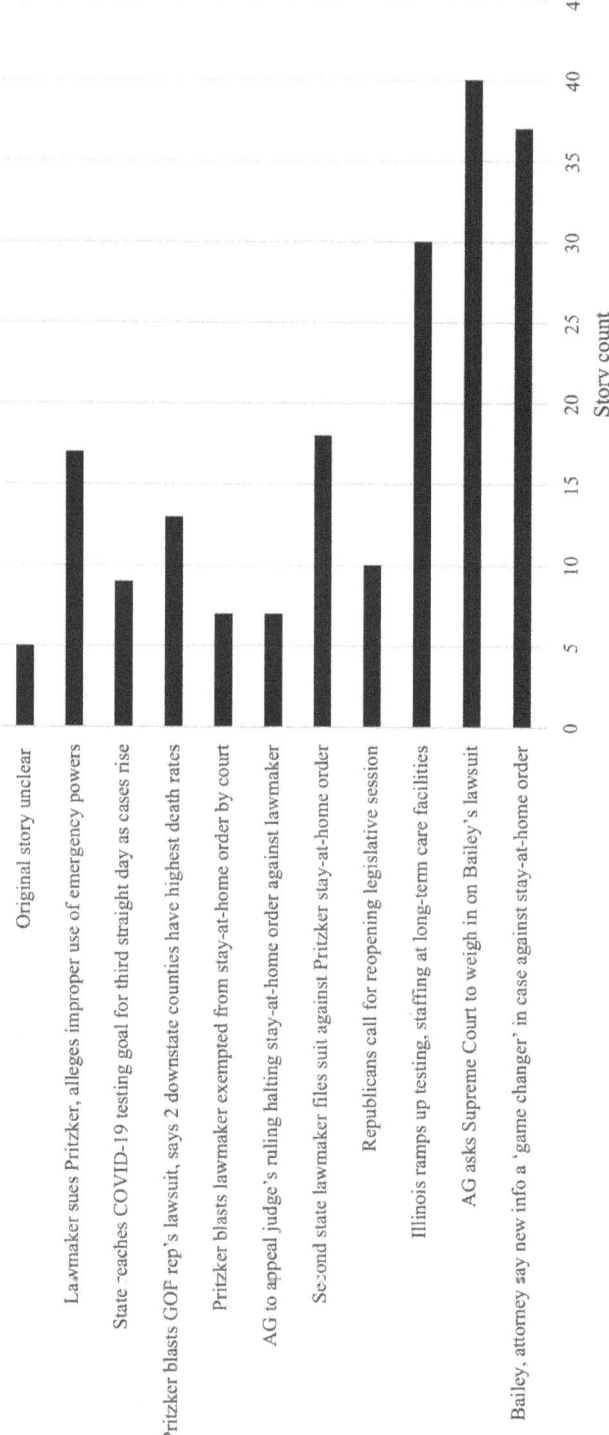

Figure 9 Count of syndicated stories from *Capitol News Illinois*.

Amplifying Extremism 47

Table 2 Syndicated stories from Shaw Media

Date	Syndicated story	Story count
April 27	Judge rules against Pritzker's stay-at-home order in downstate Illinois	27
April 28	Pritzker calls state Rep. Bailey's lawsuit a 'cheap political stunt' over stay-at-home order	28
April 28	Sen. Sue Rezin urges residents to follow safeguards until court battle plays out	1
April 29	Rep. Cabello becomes state's second lawmaker to file suit against Pritzker's stay-at-home order	28
April 29	What rate of positive COVID-19 cases do we need to hit before re-opening? Local health officials weigh in	23
May 1	Hosey: Out there just dying to reopen Illinois	1

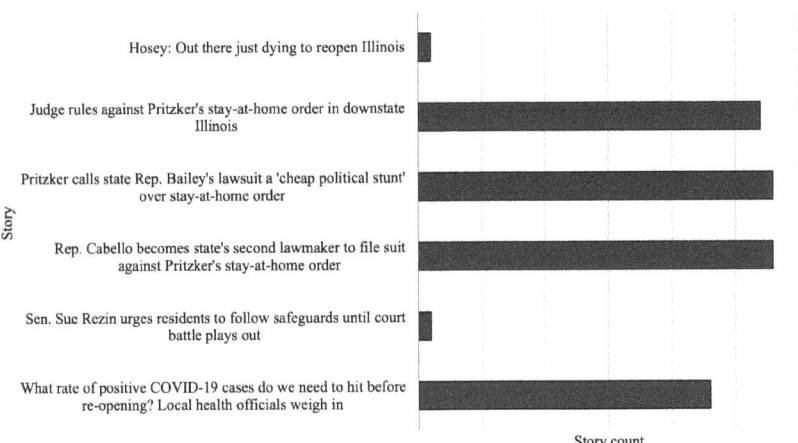

Figure 10 Count of syndicated stories from Shaw Media.

readers each month across Illinois and Iowa. It turned to three reporters to cover the Bailey story. Shaw Media's syndicated content from its State House staff was reproduced across Shaw's weekly, biweekly, and daily newspapers across Illinois. In addition, local newspapers that were not part of Shaw Media also incorporated coverage from the *Chicago Tribune* and other newspapers around the state. Figure 10 shows the stories written by Shaw Media staff writers. Of the total 108 stories, 106 are repeated with minor variations and account for 17.7 percent of the stories in the total data set. Table 2 provides a list of headlines of syndicated stories from Shaw Media.

4.4.1 Radio and Television Amplification

The structural links across public media radio also amplified Bailey's lawsuit across the state. NPR Illinois, out of Springfield, covered the story on Saturday, April 25; Northern Public Radio hosted the NPR Illinois story on its website. The affiliate, based out of Northern Illinois University in DeKalb, serves the outer ring of suburban Chicago, bringing Bailey's lawsuit to these suburban news consumers. Illinois Public Media, located in Champaign, and WBEZ, Chicago's largest public radio station, picked up the story the day of the ruling (Illinois Public Media also credits the AP for the blurb). It is hard to firmly detail any absolute evidence of intermedia agenda setting, but NPR network affiliates share story lists and lineups with other member stations and NPR itself. (Figure 11 shows the percentage of stories syndicated by medium).

Local television is anything but local, with designated market areas that go beyond state borders, as they do in Illinois; moreover, local television is widely understood to not direct much of its coverage to local politics, much less state politics. The local news outlets that stand to have wide reach – local television – seem poorly positioned to provide meaningful local news coverage. While there are limits to the number of stations any one corporation or individual can hold in a specific market, television stations are often part of two different network structures: a constellation of stations owned by the same company and the network affiliate (ABC, CBS, NBC, Fox, CW, PBS), which provides support for national programming and advertising. This network structure can facilitate an exchange of content across different geographical areas.

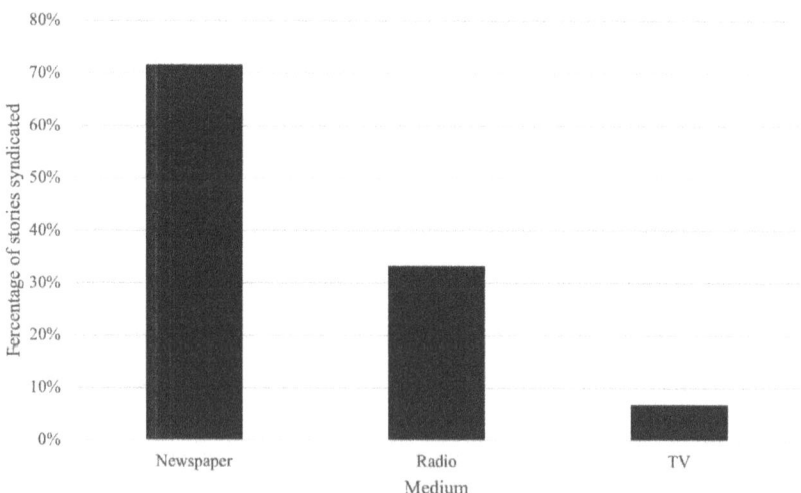

Figure 11 Percentage of stories syndicated by medium.

However, local television stations also played an important role in boosting Bailey's name recognition. While fieldwork suggests that local television coverage of political news is sparse, Bailey, as a first-term state house representative, was able to break through these limitations. Bailey announced his lawsuit in Clay County, not in Springfield, the capitol, but he did so over Facebook live, which may have given him a wider geographic reach. But the boost across the state via local television took his name and video beyond Clay County. Consider that local television station WAND hosted this Facebook live video. The NBC affiliate station is located in Decatur, in Central Illinois, and is owned by Block Communications, a privately held company known for its conservative politics; the wife of the company's owner publicly supported the insurrection on Twitter; following the insurrection, employees at Block were encouraged to downplay participant's connection to Donald Trump (Deto, 2021). Local television in the US owned by the right-wing Sinclair media conglomerate has been associated with a rightward shift in vote patterns (Levendusky, 2022). But another station also amplified Bailey's initial announcement: WISL, whose signal reaches southern Illinois, southeast Missouri, and portions of western Kentucky and Tennessee. The station is owned by Allen Communications, one of the few Black-owned companies that owns television stations. Founder Byron Allen, a Democrat donor, would later go on to malign Trump's corrosive politics. The boost cannot be just blamed on getting lucky and appearing on a conservative television station.

Bailey's first major television appearance was on Nextstar's *Capitol Connection*, broadcast out of Springfield and Champaign; although Chicago's Nexstar station, WGN, did not broadcast this as syndicated content (WGN journalist, personal communication, September 29, 2023). Within news organizations like WGN, radio, television segments, and web copy provided multiple points of entry for a news consumer of WGN to learn about Bailey's lawsuit. Notably, WTTW, Chicago's PBS station, gave Bailey some of his most extensive television coverage prior to his appearance on Fox News, with an extended cut, nineteen-minute interview on its website. Given long-standing public perceptions of liberal public media, this extended engagement with Bailey on public television is surprising.

4.4.2 Digital-First and Niche Coverage

Across the corpus, the digital-first content was the most "original" content, however, many of these stories were not original news coverage, but simply repurposing what had been covered elsewhere. This may be misleading, however.

For instance, the April 27 *Daily Caller* story has a staff byline, but it repurposes/aggregates the original reporting in the AP, adding additional commentary.

Niche political media also played an important role. CapitolFax.com is an Illinois state politics subscription-only, digital-first site established in 1998. The insider audience reading *CapitolFax* includes journalists and lawmakers alike. *CapitolFax*'s work goes beyond this insider audience; the journalist who runs the site contributed an opinion piece picked up by Illinois newspapers such as *The Daily Pantagraph* (Bloomington), the *Herald & Review* (Decatur), and the *Chicago Sun-Times* pointing to poll numbers that Illinois residents generally support Pritzker's handling of the pandemic.

The site's more contemporary and corporate version is *Politico Illinois*, under *Politico's* national politics team. As per our member-checking with *Politico*, the national editor edits the journalist responsible for *Politico Illinois* and helps determine which stories ought to break through for its national newsletters. Sustained coverage in *Politico Illinois* of Bailey elevated the significance of the story. Thus, *Politico*'s own network, via its national politics team structure, contributed to the spread of this story.

4.5 Reflections: Republican Media Coverage

Often, scholars characterize right-wing media as hyperpartisan, highly networked Republican misinformation machines – "flood the zone with shit," as Breitbart's Steve Bannon put it. But what we see in our analysis is that the mainstream news media does much of the work for right-wing news media. The objective, stenographic journalism of the AP is re-headlined and pushed out by the *Washington Times* and the *Washington Examiner*, and the stories in *The Daily Caller*, *The Daily Wire*, and *Gateway Pundit* do not provide any original reporting – just a rehashing of existing news coverage. The AP coverage works to amplify Bailey's national recognition: simply through the AP network, which includes the *Washington Examiner*, *The Washington Times*, *Breitbart*, and *The Daily Caller* alike, Bailey's name is elevated beyond Illinois. The stories set Bailey up as a crusader against Pritzker, repeating verbatim without analysis of Bailey's drum beat of liberty and freedom and his insistence that the issue was not COVID restrictions per se, but constitutional overreach. All that the right-wing outlets had to do was simply to repurpose the AP's coverage in order to amplify Bailey – changing nothing but the headlines. Bailey's Fox News appearance comes after the bulk of mainstream media coverage and conservative digital-first and newspaper coverage – suggesting that these smaller outlets may have an agenda-setting role for Fox itself. But notably, the *Washington Times* and *Washington Examiner* did not engage in misinformation;

the misinformation-rife *Daily Mail* featured local coverage that surfaced Republican politicians who otherwise were not party to any of the lawsuits or the action directly.

Also noteworthy and deserving of additional research are the connections between local and national right-wing content. The smaller Edgar County/Illinois Leaks does not appear to have much impact on other coverage – it is mostly links out to legal documents. However, the connection between other locally reported Illinois stories and the right-wing national news media is murkier. In the first corpus-building exercise, the stories in the *Washington Times* and *Washington Examiner* that were not AP stories were credited with a *Center Square: Illinois* attribution. *Center Square* is a GOP-funded nonprofit news digital-first site. But four months later, we did a second compilation of our corpus for auditing purposes, and the taglines crediting *Center Square* from the *Washington Times* and *Washington Examiner* disappeared from the articles. The search index within Center Square Illinois does not extend back into its 2020 archives, creating further uncertainty. This may be because additional scrutiny has come over *Center Square's* role in the conservative news network for pumping "pink slime" misinformation into local news ecologies. While during the 2022 gubernatorial election, Darren Bailey's political stock had risen enough to be promoted through AI-generated stories through right-wing owned "pink slime" news websites (Wenzel, 2023), this was not the case in 2020, as Bailey was bursting on the scene. Still, both local and national partisan news outlets featured local, on-the-ground reporting based in communities of coverage of local politicians that stakeholders concerned with the future of news might consider more carefully before discounting.

As a whole, when public stakeholders worry about the decline of news, they are likely imagining that geographically-specific news outlets are producing original coverage for and about a particular locale. However, this idea of original, location-specific, audience-specific coverage is an ideal that does not bear out in the reality of our corpus. Whether by linked ownership, content sharing, some sort of network relationship (like public media outlets), or wire syndication, the corpus of news stories is highly homogenous. The same or nearly similar content is appearing in dozens of outlets, irrespective of whether the content was on television, radio, or in newspapers, with limited customization for geographically proximate audiences, which might have been all the more important during COVID-19. Almost three-quarters of newspaper stories were syndicated/duplicated content appearing in different sources along with more than a quarter of all radio stories. Not only was Bailey's name being repeated throughout the state and the country, giving him a tremendous boost in potential name recognition, but he also benefited from coverage that focused on framing the lawsuit as a novel story and a contest between an unknown upstart Republican from rural America and a big-time Democrat governor in a "blue" state. These news values, discussed in the next section, obscured the potential extremist threat that a politician like Bailey presented to Illinois. The consequences of this coverage had reverberations for the state's political culture for years to come.

5 Journalists, New Norms, and Amplifying Extremism

Section 3 of this monograph addressed the first research question: what are the features of local political ecologies that might facilitate the rise of small town extremists? – focusing primarily on the structural and cultural elements of the political and media ecosystems in Illinois. In Section 4, we sought to provide a descriptive overview of "how" via an analysis of aggregate coverage patterns and links between and across news outlets. We pointed to moments that we think explain the surges and duration of the coverage itself. We also began our initial analysis of our second research question: How do the practices and challenges facing the news industry – local, regional, national, and partisan media – serve to amplify extremism? In this section, Section 5, we consider how the routine work of American journalism at the national, state, and local levels might accidentally optimize the spread of extremism and create space for the tolerance of illiberal politics in the public sphere more generally. Here, how standard, professional norms of reporting structured news coverage in ways that legitimized Bailey. Across the corpus of our data, three main news values drive the continued coverage of Bailey: objectivity, journalists' focus on covering "knowns," and conflict.

5.1 News Values: Limits of Objectivity

As discussed in Section 1, journalism studies scholars have critiqued the practice of objectivity as leading to stenographic coverage. Practices of defensive professionalism remove journalists from assigning causality, asserting blame, or offering direct opinions (Usher, 2019); Tuchman (1972) called objectivity a "strategic ritual" as journalists turn to quotations as a way to defer judgment, turning instead to experts and sources to provide verification, either through quotations or turning to the authority of institutions and organizations for the "facts" needed to craft the story. Journalism's "view from nowhere" can lead to a false balance between two sides that lack equal claims to fact-based reality or are represented unequally in proportion to the actual strength of support for a particular viewpoint (Callison & Young, 2019).

Similarly, the standard inverted pyramid with the five w's (and one h): who, what, what, where, when, how – but not why – keeps the focus on presentism and action rather than context. Carey (1974) argues that these "canons" – "rules of news selection, judgment, and writing" – in turn "define what is considered to be real" (p. 247).

Almost the entire corpus of our data consists of straight news coverage drawn from interviews or press conferences. Our corpus features only a handful of opinion pieces and editorials: the *Chicago Tribune* editorial, a column, an opinion piece, the *Wall Street Journal* opinion, and an opinion piece from CapitolFax that ran in the *Sun-Times* and in some local newspapers. Other than Bailey's appearance on Fox, which was essentially Bailey's investiture as a power player in Illinois politics – the culmination of days of coverage – Bailey's first burst into a larger public role is not the result of right-wing agitation, loud opinion journalism, and hyperpartisan (mis)information. Rather, Bailey's reputation gets built up from stenographic coverage that positions Bailey as the defender of liberty and justice against the encroachment of the state.

The initial coverage of Bailey's lawsuit stenographically recorded his justification for the lawsuit: "Enough is enough! I filed this lawsuit on behalf of myself and my constituents who are ready to go back to work and resume a normal life" and some local television and local newspapers carried the Facebook live video and accompanying stories without even mentioning Pritzker and failing to carry a response. On April 23, Bailey's video announcing his lawsuit appeared on the website of WAND; the 178-word story accompanying the video followed with stenographic coverage, a play-by-play of the politician's announcement:

> CLAY COUNTY, Ill. (WAND) – State Representative Darren Bailey said he has filed a lawsuit against the Illinois governor and his stay-at-home order.
>
> He said he heard from his district about the concern of continuing the Illinois stay-at-home.
>
> Bailey believes the governor has overextended his powers by extending the order. In the lawsuit Bailey claims Pritzker doesn't have the authority to issue emergency orders for a period of time more than thirty days from the declaration of the disaster.
>
> "We can't be held hostage by this," Bailey said in a Facebook live video he posted after filing the lawsuit.
>
> He said it's wrong and requires action.

Additional bylined coverage is provided by WSIL, another local television station, headlined "Illinois lawmaker files suit over governor's stay at home order." The bylined story is similarly anodyne and repeats verbatim Bailey's

Facebook live video, including Rep. Bailey's critique of Pritzker's legitimacy... "... the unprecedented power and authority he wields under the current crisis calls for an immediate review and reconsideration of legislative intent." The article does distinguish the specificities of the lawsuit, noting it is a complaint that includes a request for a temporary restraining order and preliminary injunction, with links to both, but offers no direct quote from the governor's office nor any information about the COVID pandemic.

The AP's first story coverage of the lawsuit, in a story filed from Louisville, Illinois, home to the Clay County Court House, repeats Bailey's claims without quotations: "Pritzker has exceeded his authority and is violating the civil rights of the state's residents." This article, however, does quote Pritzker, "I know how badly we all want our normal lives back." and encouraging residents to "dig in." The 275-word story concludes with a direct quote from Bailey challenging Pritzker's authority, also repeated in the other stories, saying the move "calls for an immediate review and reconsideration of legislative intent."

On April 25, Bailey's lawsuit was picked up by NPR Illinois, the NPR station headquartered in Springfield. The text story begins with Bailey's arguments against Pritzker, in a similar stenographic account:

> "An Illinois Republican is suing Governor J. B. Pritzker over restrictions he's put in place to combat the new coronavirus pandemic."
>
> State Rep. Darren Bailey (Xenia) alleges the governor does not have the power to keep the state under a stay-at-home order and disaster proclamation, as he moved to do this week.

As the lawsuit picked up steam in news coverage, Bailey's arguments continue to be reported as quotes or paraphrases, but there is little substance to ground or counter his claims. While the *Sun-Times* provides context that Bailey is part of a group of state legislators who once voted to kick Chicago out of the state, his justification for the lawsuit goes unchallenged: "I saw it as a victory for the people, for the Constitution that I believe has been hijacked here in Illinois," Bailey said. In an interview with *Politico*, Bailey similarly stressed the constitutional angle: "Instead the governor is making those determinations.... To let something like this go on slowly degrades our constitutional rights. That's what I'm after." The AP lede on April 27, the day of the ruling, specifically mentions Bailey's claim that the stay-at-home "exceeds [Pritzker's] emergency authority and violates individual civil rights." The second paragraph refers to Pritzker's order as "the Democratic governor's far-reaching executive decree." Chicago PBS station WTTW's pull quote for its interview with Bailey is reminiscent of a Trump tweet: "The governor accused me of being responsible for millions of people dying," Bailey said. "That was sad." The judge issuing the ruling described Pritzker as having "shredded the constitution," a phrase Bailey began using in subsequent interviews.

The *Washington Post* also quoted Bailey verbatim without context that might challenge the lawsuits' claims: "The governor was just clearly overreaching his authority and his power." John Cabello, who filed the second lawsuit against the governor, offered the news media an even more provocative quote, "He's acting like a dictator, not a governor," although only the *Chicago Tribune* noted his role as head of the Trump reelection campaign in Illinois. *USA Today*'s brief on April 30th described the new lawsuit: "his will benefit everyone in the state" and includes the quote, "I want to see everyone get back to a normal, American way of life." But there is no contrast with death numbers, the account of full hospitals, or any other counter to these claims.

The right-wing press also picked up on this language of "liberty." *Gateway Pundit* focused its coverage on executive overreach, with the headline, "Judge Rules Illinois Governor Exceeded Authority, Violated Civil Rights with Coronavirus Stay-at-Home Order." The *Washington Times* also added additional critique of Pritzker to its April 27th AP coverage, "The ruling came the same day House Republicans attacked Pritzker on another front, renewing demands for details on state prison inmates released early because of COVID-19 fears." With Laura Ingraham on Fox on April 29, Bailey casts himself as an unlikely hero standing up against oppression: "I say we've seen this happen many times throughout history, even the history of our great nation. It takes one person to stand up on a wrong."

None of these stories published in right-wing media contain misinformation about COVID or Illinois politics. On April 30, the *WSJ* published an op-ed by Illinois State Senator Dan McConchie supporting Bailey's cause:

> As governors across the country destroy their states' economies in the name of public health, there is shockingly little oversight of their actions.
>
> In my state of Illinois, Gov. J. B. Pritzker has locked down the state, closing swaths of commerce and limiting the movement of citizens in response to COVID-19. These actions have been challenged in court by my colleague, state Rep. Darren Bailey, and a judge initially agreed to a temporary restraining order on the governor's emergency measure, but only as they apply to Mr. Bailey. The rest of the state remains under lockdown by the governor's orders, which continue without oversight.

While an opinion piece is by definition an opinion, the willingness of the *WSJ* to publish this piece pushing back against a lack of government oversight points to the reorientation of the lawsuit beyond COVID, enabling politicians to avoid being called out for flaunting public health measures as a politicking.

Notably, a scandal that made some news among right-wing news outlets and activist groups did not become a scandal in the mainstream media: that Pritzker's own wife was violating the stay-at-home order by traveling to Florida. But her travel did happen, and perhaps norms of consensus and balance in journalism or Pritzker's unwillingness to verbally confirm the visits limited mainstream news reporting on this. Perhaps, consciously or unconsciously, mainstream journalists did not wish to further undermine the governor's credibility to ask Illinois residents to "dig in," but this news did not become a dominant storyline. Later in the pandemic, such two-sided/hypocritical stories of politicians doing what they told others to avoid doing (Nancy Pelosi getting a haircut without a mask; Gavin Newsom holding a birthday dinner party) did generate more headlines outside of just the right-wing ecosystem. In mainstream news media, however, Bailey is the main focus of the story, and the news outlets reporting on "straight" news do not push back on his claims, merely repeat them. The supposed objectivity and view from nowhere and the distancing of journalists from taking a position have been the subject of enduring critique both from inside and outside the profession.

5.2 Amplification: Coverage of "Knowns" and News Values of Conflict

Routine coverage of known figures and known institutions, principally elected political figures, organizes news production – structurally, beats are devoted to following around powerful people – with the president of the US as the iconic "known." In state and local news, however, the governor becomes the key figure of attention. What Pritzker says and does gets covered as a matter of routine newswork; Pritzker held almost daily news briefings with the press and with open question-and-answer sessions during the initial weeks and months of the pandemic. Bailey benefited from this routine coverage: the more Pritzker engaged with the lawsuit and Bailey, the more attention Bailey received. News routines also help structure coverage: While journalists cannot predict exactly what will happen on any given day, they do know that the governor is going to do *something* and whatever it is, because he's the governor, it is news. But there is perfunctory coverage of the day-to-day and the more interesting, "man bites dog" story – and Bailey likely benefited from journalists eager to cover news beyond the number of COVID cases and the governor promising to do his best. When it comes to routine coverage, novelty can help drive interest to the stories, both for journalists competing for attention and prestige within their own newsrooms, and for focusing the attention of news audiences. A disgruntled politician hoping to sue the governor is not on its own terms novelty, but the context of COVID-19 itself made the lawsuit distinctive: a governor in a big blue state and liberal stronghold was being challenged by an upstart, unknown Republican state representative – in one of the first challenges of its kind. That the judges' ruling only applied to Bailey drove additional attention to the story: the first major challenge to COVID restrictions didn't overhaul the restrictions, just whether Bailey could be forced to follow them – adding further "man bites dog" aura to the story.

For example, the *Washington Post's* coverage profiled the lawmaker, with a large photo outside the State House provided by Bailey, and a lead that pointed to the outcome of the lawsuit, "As some Republicans seeking to reopen the economy launch a full-court press against stay-at-home restrictions, one GOP lawmaker in Illinois scored an unusual legal victory on Monday – for himself." *CNN*'s story also focused on this "twist" in the court decision and anti-COVID mitigation, with the headline: "Judge grants Illinois lawmaker a personal exemption from state's stay-at-home order." Conservative media also picked up on the added interest in the ruling, too. *The Daily Wire* focused on the novelty of the lawsuit and the subsequent decision, "Illinois Judge Halts Governor's Stay-At-Home Order ... Sort Of." The article's lead reports Bailey's lawsuit "An Illinois judge has granted a temporary stay against Governor J. B. Pritzker's extension [sic] of the state's coronavirus related stay-at-home order, marking the first time a state court has weighed in on the constitutionality of stay-at-home orders at large."

5.2.1 Conflict

Conflict is an enduring news value: journalists use conflict to "weigh in" or "intervene" in events, debates, or analysis (Bartholomé, Lecheler & De Vreese, 2018). While this is seemingly contradictory with the view from nowhere, the conflict frame actually enables journalistic detachment as journalists can cast the principal actors against each other, backgrounding their own role in assessing newsworthiness. When it comes to political journalism, conflict is most often operationalized as the "horse race," with candidates or power struggles between branches of government. The portrayal of conflict in the news may be actually disproportionate relative to the actual political reality of the power dynamics of the conflict itself. Within this context of journalists using conflict to frame stories, two main themes emerged as points of contention: the battle between Pritzker and Bailey, and the larger, cultural disconnect between Chicago and its collar counties and downstate/rural Illinois.

5.2.2 Winners and Losers

The win/loss contest is buttressed by events: in this case, there was indeed a win (for Bailey) and a loss (for Pritzker), with each new politician announcing a lawsuit adding further support for Bailey and fuel to the fight against Pritzker. On April 24, 2020, WBEZ, the Chicago public radio station carried an extensive text story featuring the governor's justification for the extension of the stay-at-home order; Pritzker obliquely defended his stay-at-home order without mentioning Bailey. Pritzker is quoted: "No amount of political pressure would ever make me allow such a scenario for our state, our beloved state of Illinois," he said. "So, the numbers present us with only one choice." The source of the political pressure, however, was coming from Bailey. On April 27, the *Reuters* story spun the case as having potential implications beyond Illinois, broadening the potential appeal of the story, not just as a win for Bailey but also as headwinds of other battles headed Pritzker's way: "A state lawmaker in Illinois won a restraining order on Monday against Governor J. B. Pritzker's stay-at-home orders in a case that could lead to more legal challenges against decrees by the first- term governor intended to stem the spread of COVID-19."

The AP quoted Pritzker directly confronting Bailey's actions: "It's insulting. It's dangerous and people's safety and health have now been put at risk," Pritzker said. "There may be people who contract coronavirus as a result of what Darren Bailey has done."

Also on April 27, NPR affiliate story characterizes the governor's reaction as: "Pritzker lashed out at him during the briefing." The *Sun-Times*' lede begins, "Stinging from the burn of a judge's ruling ..." and describes how Pritzker "opened his daily briefing with a verbal attack on state Rep. Darren Bailey." Pritzker tells the press that Bailey's lawsuit is

> "a cheap political stunt designed so that the representative can see his name in headlines, and unfortunately, he has briefly been successful in that most callous of feats."

And in the follow-up coverage on April 28, *Politico Illinois* compares the conflict to winning a football game:

> The stay-at-home order to combat the coronavirus has become a big political football for Gov. J. B. Pritzker and other state leaders around the country.

Politico characterized Pritzker's response to Bailey's lawsuit in his daily briefing as "lengthy," legitimating the significance of the conflict.

The right also used the conflict to propel the story nationally. On April 28, The *Washington Times* again published two stories, with one headline focusing on Pritzker "Stay at home lawsuit a 'stunt.'" The *Washington Examiner* published two stories (repurposed from *Center Square*) quoting Kankakee sheriff Mike Downey. "What they do in their social life obviously dictates where they're going healthwise," Downey said. "For him to blame sheriffs, which doesn't surprise me, is irresponsible," adding, "I just don't see it being legitimate." The Examiner ran a second bylined story, subtitled "'Shredded the Constitution': Illinois judge rules against governor's stay-at-home extension." There is no obvious misinformation about COVID-19 or any of the political positions in right-wing news.

Bailey's appearance on Fox on April 29 strengthened his position as *the* Republican challenging Pritzker's power. Ingraham heralded the first-term representative for his bravery in challenging Pritzker:

You as a first-term representative were actually doing what you're supposed to do and actually what some journalists are supposed to do …

> And you find out this order only has legitimacy for 30 days, OK?.
> Again, you, a first-term representative figured this out.

That same day, a Fox file photo of Bailey accompanied an unrelated opinion piece by an Illinois state legislator arguing against federal relief funds for COVID due to the state's corruption problems. Much of the coverage over the next few days would go on to frame the conflict more broadly moving beyond Bailey to a broader clash between Republicans and Democrats in the state, but Bailey's lawsuit is the catalyst for the conflict.

5.2.3 Rural–Urban Divides

The urban–rural divides between downstate and Chicagoland (discussed in Section 3 as the structural and cultural elements of the PMP political ecology) reflect an enduring sense of disempowerment and frustration among downstate residents who feel ignored or even harmed by Chicago-area Democrats. This emerges as a secondary sub-theme within the larger conflict framing. On April 23, when Bailey announced his suit, his hometown paper, the *Effingham Daily News*, provided additional coverage of Bailey beyond his Facebook live video. The politician invokes the rural/urban power dynamic, noting, "They're the ones that really hold the power when it comes to a health crisis or situation." On April 27, The *Chicago Sun-Times* provided more insight into Bailey's downstate politics, reporting that the politician was a "vocal supporter" of Trump and part of a bloc of state Republicans who "once sponsored legislation to kick Chicago out of Illinois." Bailey also told the *Sun-Times*, "We're not affected by the COVID crisis like the other parts of the state are." The *Chicago Tribune* editorializes against Bailey, but also legitimizes the downstate frustration. Headlined "Pritzker's stay-home order in question. Win for downstate, setback for overall public health," the editorial describes the ongoing events as "a rebellion": "The rebellion has been brewing.... We understand the financial, tax and spending decisions that often are driven by the interests of the most populous regions of the state ... But public health is a different story." Bailey's actions are a form of rebellion by downstate against upstate, and the *Tribune* legitimizes the anger and rationale, but not the attack.

On April 27, WGN Radio, a commercial radio station in Chicago, hosted Bailey for a twelve-minute interview with its midday host, with "He explains why irreparable harm would amount from keeping the town closed" appended as the description to the audio file. On April 28, when Pritzker filed notice of an appeal against the ruling, both local and national coverage highlighted some of these rural–urban divides. In an extended interview with WTTW, Chicago's public television station, Bailey invokes urban–rural differences rather than any anti-science rationale for his beef with Pritzker: "It doesn't mean we go rampant," Bailey said, "This is about a local control, and obeying the law, versus what our governor chooses to do." WCIA local television carried a story focused on other rural politicians contesting the stay-at-home order, with the text headline, "We will not enforce compliance to the demise of our businesses." The lede points to the forgotten and powerless downstate politicians, "The mayor and city council of Farmer City don't necessarily expect a response to the letter they sent to Governor J. B. Pritzker on Tuesday – but then again, that wasn't entirely the point," and quotes the mayor ".what's good for upstate is not necessarily good for downstate." This too turns the framing of the conflict as justified based on the rural differences in a larger power struggle.

National outlets also pointed to Bailey's rural roots.

> From *The Post*: "The governor was just clearly overreaching his authority and his powers," Bailey, a farmer who represents a rural district in southern Illinois, told *The Washington Post*.

NPR's story similarly focuses on the battle between a Republican and a Democrat, one rural and the other cosmopolitan, and therefore disconnected from nonurban areas:

> The fight over COVID-19 has become a legal battle in Illinois, pitting a Republican state lawmaker from a rural county against the Democratic governor.
>
> Darren Bailey argued the state's latest stay-at-home order was taking an unfair economic toll on his constituents in Clay County. So he sued last week. And won. Sort of.

On May 1, when anti-Pritzker protests happened in Springfield and Chicago, the *Chicago Tribune* ran a story, "People are frightened': Across rural Illinois, economic frustrations mix with anxiety over COVID-19," describing the contradictory fears of COVID and of economic problems and cites the case of a woman who backs Bailey because of her "economic anxiety and her dissatisfaction with Pritzker" for being too focused on Chicago. The "contradiction" is between two possible ends of livelihood: financial ruin and mortality – and both fears are validated by the coverage, legitimizing the downstate narrative that closings are disempowering them even further.

The conflict frame is largely critiqued for focusing on personalities rather than ideas, and thus, limiting public knowledge about the underlying stakes or consequences of various policy alternatives. Journalists took advantage of the narrative arcs of a small town Republican politician versus a big-time Democrat governor, and this conflict frame helped drive the competing claims forward into additional coverage. Setting Pritzker against Bailey as the latest example of "political football" as per *Politico,* turns the story into a battle of personalities rather than a battle between two people with opposite commitments to the rule of law and democratic processes.

As a whole, Bailey benefited from news coverage across state, national, local, and regional news media that boosted his name recognition nationally, statewide, and within the Republican party. This splash of coverage points to the vulnerabilities of American journalism to extremist capture. Journalists' commitment to objectivity can leave out important context that helps situate the larger stakes beyond the day's reporting. Today's novel "man bites dog" extremist story may have a novel set of facts, but extremist challenges to the rule of law have become routine stories themselves. Moreover, the focus on neutrality can result in a false balance, giving more emphasis and legitimation to people and positions that actually do not have this wider support. Routine coverage of politicians can result in similar problems: if Pritzker mentions a politician, even if not directly by name, it is newsworthy and that politician gets some inadvertent shine. Finally, a focus on conflict has a similar downside: personalities rather than issues take center stage, setting up the coverage as a conflict may overemphasize the credibility of the issue or event behind the conflict. The "rebellion" that Bailey initiated, as per the *Chicago Tribune*, seems tame in comparison to the actual effort at rebellion that would come on January 6, 2021.

6 Avoiding Accidental Amplification

This Element sought to elucidate how extremists are amplified in the contemporary US media and political ecologies, going beyond the national-level context to consider how local and state extremists are able to publicize their causes and gain momentum. Our focus on the case of a small town state house representative, Darren Bailey, offers an important snapshot into the dynamics that shape the rise of other politicians and antidemocratic causes to national prominence. The ascent of extremist politicians can happen in a matter of days; copycat politicians follow, and members of the public may be emboldened to engage in antidemocratic advocacy or even violence. During the ten days under study, Bailey sued Pritzker, was featured on a segment on Fox News and in an op-ed in the *WSJ*, and protesters against COVID-19 restrictions were spotted carrying Nazi slogans. While we do not aim to draw causal inferences between political actors, media coverage, and public antidemocratic expression, the microscopic approach can provide important insights that studies that employ larger datasets and more lawmakers cannot. We asked two main research questions:

1) What are the features of local political ecologies that might facilitate the rise of small town antidemocratic extremists?
2) How might journalism itself – the profession's practices and norms, the structure of the news industry itself, and underlying economic incentives – serve to amplify these bad actors?

In Section 1, we overviewed the three theoretical approaches that guided our empirical work: the PMP framework, media storms scholarship, and the political economy of the news media – specifically how economics and news values shape media coverage. In Section 2, we discussed the methodology for our case study and our corpus construction. In Section 3, we addressed the first research question, with the PMP approach guiding our use of interviews, fieldwork, and secondary source material to detail the underlying political and media ecologies that backgrounded Bailey's ascent. In Sections 4 and 5, we addressed the second research question. We examined the structure of the news ecology to understand the dynamics within the coverage across different news media and categories of sources, and considered how news coverage, through the routine practices and values of professional journalists, may facilitate the accidental amplification of extremism and, in turn, make space for illiberal politics. In this concluding section, we highlight our most surprising findings putting them in conversation with extant theory and address some of the limitations of our approach. We end by reckoning with how this case highlights the tension between extremism and the role of the news media in covering what has become an increasingly routine narrative: a small town politician making it big, and quickly, for the latest "man bites dog" click-bait controversy.

6.1 Cross-Media Corpus Construction and the Descriptive Approach

Our research showcases the importance and strength of cross-media, cross-database corpus construction in political communication scholarship. Our study was intentionally descriptive: we wanted to understand how the news media – broadly understood – might play a role in amplifying extremist voices, especially in light of declines in local newspapers and the rise and maturation of a hyperpartisan right-wing media ecosystem. We also wanted to offer a contextual understanding of the political dynamics that make places vulnerable to extremist capture. Bailey's seemingly sudden rise from first-term, unknown state rep. to a segment on Fox News was in part what drew our attention to his particular case. A focus on this ten-day period enabled us to provide a turn-by-turn analysis of the case as it developed and to feel confident that our corpus construction was comprehensive. We will not claim it is absolutely complete, but the corpus is far more comprehensive than the typical representative sampling/database-driven corpus construction approach to content analysis.

We aimed to create a replicable approach to doing retrospective corpus creation that would optimize for the array of outlets and media for a specific research query. We knew we could not just rely on national news to create our corpus, as our focus was on a local politician. To this end, we combined different library databases (both proprietary and the Internet Archive), organic web searches, targeted website searching, and social media searches, which enabled us to construct a retrospective corpus with a non-duplicate sample of 596 different stories of Bailey's rise over our ten-day period. We incorporated a vast diversity of source content: digital-first outlets, local, local-partisan, national, and Republican digital-first; local television from across the state of Illinois through transcripts and web-text stories on their pages; weekly and daily newspapers, including some that were not archived as part of library databases for state and local newspapers; and beyond. Local television and digital-first sites are rarely contained within proprietary databases, but open web searches provide a starting list from which to dig deeper at the source level.

Our descriptive approach also underscores the importance of fieldwork and interview data for political communication research. This Element used the PMP framework to foreground the preexisting political and media context that led to Bailey's rise. Structurally, Illinois politics were becoming increasingly politically polarized and geographically divided between Democrat-majority Chicago/Chicagoland and the Republican rest of the state; Republicans were disempowered due to majoritarian Democratic party representative rule and were set to be further disempowered through congressional redistricting. The situational context of COVID-19 presented an immediate shock to the political ecosystem; the seriousness of the pandemic was quickly politicized with Republicans chafing against the science of the pandemic and restrictions to curb the virus. Taken together, our corpus construction, fieldwork, and interview data gave us the ability to track possible relationships across stories appearing in different outlets, reconstruct the flow of news content, and interpret these findings in light of the on-the-ground, materially situated context. Our approach provided a counterpoint to common assumptions about the relationship between state, local, and national press/politics, the performance of right-wing media, and concerns about the loss of local news media. These include:

1. *Local news coverage is highly redundant: outlet diversity is not content diversity, and efforts to rebuild local coverage may have unanticipated consequences*
2. *The absence of misinformation on right-wing sites and the presence of originally reported coverage*
3. *The importance of national media and local broadcast television in amplifying Bailey*

6.2 Outlet Diversity and Content Diversity

Scholars of the political economy of news media often champion the importance of robust, geographically specific local news outlets and decry media consolidation, arguing that outlet diversity and ownership diversity provide more robust coverage (Pickard, 2019). Stakeholders worry about declines in state house news coverage and how this might affect public knowledge and accountability, but syndicated, identical content that appears across dozens of different outlets does not reflect the pluralism in coverage that a robust local news ecosystem might ideally offer. Many of the current policy efforts to strengthen local news involve shoring up the economic foundations of local newspapers. Historically small local newspapers provided unique, distinct coverage of their communities. Still, news outlets are not always first to the story, nor can they be counted upon to provide original and/or superior coverage compared to other general interest, nonlocal news organizations.

Still, our findings show that newspapers do provide the vast majority of coverage about Bailey's lawsuit, reflecting many studies that point to the importance of local newspapers in providing original content to their communities. Almost 80 percent of our corpus is from newspapers (state, local, national, and international). However, while Illinois' local newspapers remain fairly robust in quantity, these local newspapers are not offering distinct, original coverage of state politics. *Capitol News Illinois* was created to fill a gap in state house news coverage and any member of the state press association could use its reporting in their outlet: this meant that Bailey's name could be pushed out to about 460 different Illinois news outlets at no cost to the news outlet. We also saw this duplication happen across Shaw Media newspapers, a large, privately owned newspaper chain that relied on a small state house bureau for coverage for all of its newspapers.

Notably, out of our 596 stories:

~343 or 57.6 percent are syndicated from other sources – the stories do not reflect distinct news coverage uniquely tailored to a specific audience or geography.

Both national news outlets and local news outlets turned to syndicated content – either because of links across ownership or through deliberate syndication agreements, such as with the AP or *Capitol News Illinois* supplementing state house news coverage. *Capitol News Illinois* accounted for 195 of these stories, but only represented 11 different original stories, mostly placed in local newspapers. Shaw Media comprised 108 stories in our corpus but this number only reflects six different original stories. The outlets may be geographically local, but the coverage is not different – for example, one county gets the same content as the next county, albeit under a different newspaper banner name.

~ 338 of the 543 local stories (62 percent of our corpus), *were syndicated from elsewhere –* in other words, these were not originally bylined stories by the outlet itself. Stories syndicated from *Capitol News Illinois* and by Shaw Media account for 303 total stories, or 50.8 percent of the stories in our corpus overall.

~Three headlines with minor variations alone account for 111 stories in our corpus or 18.6 percent of our total. These headlines, then, were setting up the framing of the case and helped to amplify and direct attention to specific dimensions of the lawsuit.

This amplification meant that stories about an unknown downstate politician were catapulted across the geography of the state, giving Bailey's name recognition a boost.

6.2.1 Right-Wing Media: No Misinformation, Shoe-Leather Reporting

Extremist GOP media poses additional challenges to American democracy, but this scholarship shows that it is important not to dismiss partisan coverage as misinformation or lacking in news value. Public stakeholders have become concerned about local right-wing "pink slime" journalism that disguises misinformation and partisan talking points by posing as standard-bearer local news organizations (Wenzel et al., 2023). In this case, the original reporting from mainstream news media was taken up by right-wing news media; the on-the-ground coverage of the institutional news media was the critical ingredient for the fact-based fodder republished or recontextualized by partisan news organizations. *Simply republishing AP stories for right-leaning audiences provided fuel for Bailey's growing reputation.* In addition to mainstream news coverage, the GOP media coverage of Bailey emerged first in digital-first outlets like the *Daily Wire*, the *Daily Caller, Breitbart*, and the *Washington Times* and

Washington Examiner, Republican national newspapers, and culminated in his appearance on Fox – and the coverage was driven by facts, not conspiracy. We also were able to see branches of the larger story that did not gain traction, specifically the Breitbart story about Pritzker's wife leaving the state during the Safer-at-Home order.

Surprisingly, some Republican local and regional news outlets are actually providing supplemental, fact-based, "shoe leather" reporting that goes beyond the efforts of local news media. In this case, the Republican-backed news nonprofit, *Center Square Illinois* featured original coverage, quoting Republican state and local politicians who echoed Bailey's resistance. This content was picked up by the right-wing *Washington Examiner* and the *Washington Times*, a syndication approach to supplemental news coverage not unlike *Capital News Illinois*. Tracking these associations over time is difficult and harder to verify due to poor indexing by Google News and on-site search archives; future work needs to account for this challenge.

6.2.2 National Media, Broadcast Television, and Other Boosters

The diminished capacity of local and state news outlets, especially cutbacks to newspapers, does not mean that there are no journalists paying attention. We did not expect to see national media coverage. But our research suggests that national news outlets with small state and local footprints may provide the first line of reporting on stories about state politics. In fact, AP coverage was present from day one – April 23, 2020, the day the lawsuit was announced. This meant that from the get-go, Bailey's name and his antics had the potential of a global footprint – and this AP coverage was also repurposed by the right-wing national newspapers, boosting Bailey's profile in national party circles. While the AP has recently lost major clients such as Gannett newspapers, the AP still has bureaus in every state house and 231 bureaus in 93 countries. (Associated Press, n.d.). National digital-first outlets like *Politico* have set up more focused state-specific and local coverage; there are even Republican-backed nonprofit news outlets like *Center Square* whose state politics focus is then shared with larger, national partisan news organizations.

In our fieldwork and interviews, community leaders maligned the decline of rigorous local newspaper coverage of politics in their communities. They pointed to local television as limited due to its geographically ambiguous market area and its generally incomplete coverage of civic information. So, we were surprised that two local television news stations were present from the beginning. While the television outlets just repurposed Bailey's Facebook video, they had content that *Capitol News Illinois* did not offer until a full day later. As discussed, this was not just a case of a Republican-backed television news station giving airtime to a favored politician. In fact, some of the most extensive television coverage came from a Chicago PBS network station, which aired a nineteen-minute interview with Bailey, legitimizing his credibility for a public television audience. Local television markets in rural areas can cross multiple state borders, meaning local politics may not be immediately relevant to people watching the news but a politician on the news has the potential to reach a far wider geographic distribution. Moreover, local television coverage may also serve to give a local politician media experience before breaking out nationally; Bailey also got additional "practice" for his big Fox News debut thanks to these local television opportunities. Bailey's arguments were amplified through ordinary journalism, boosting his name recognition and creating discursive space for other challenges to COVID regulations – as well as other, later attacks on democratic norms.

6.3 Extremism, Illiberalism, and American Journalism

The COVID lockdown is increasingly a distant memory for many, but what it set in motion reverberates today: what was far-right pre-COVID is now the mainstay politics of Republicans serving in local, state, and national public service. More recently, it has become clear that understanding how local and state extremists gain power is highly relevant – especially given the resurgence of the right-wing culture war: GOP efforts to ban books, pass legislation restricting the activities of LGBTQ+ people, and capitalize on Roe vs. Wade's overruling. The constitutional sheriff's movement may be of particular concern going forward as the power behind anti-immigration politics grows. The movement has ties to white nationalist groups such as the Oath Keepers, and adherents believe that sheriffs have the ultimate local authority in their jurisdictions (Wippell, 2024). Journalists need to proceed with caution in order to avoid amplifying the influence of these local extremists. More broadly, news coverage serves as an institutional sign-off that a person or event or policy matters for public knowledge. The antics of these politicians have become routine news coverage, although they are often covered as a form of novelty, even journalistic safari-gaping ("Who are these people?" "Would you believe this?"), and ends up lending legitimacy and credibility to their efforts.

The news coverage of Bailey and his lawsuit gets at the heart of the tension between extremism and democratic norms – norms that in turn serve as the superstructure for how professional journalists cover the news. Was challenging the governor's expansion of his executive overreach extremist? Was this challenge antidemocratic? It is hard to justify how a politician who used the court system to challenge the presumptive overreach by the executive branch is acting antidemocratically. In fact, on first brush, Pritzker's emergency powers are not limited by the Constitution of the United States (unlike the president's) – and as per the Illinois Policy Institute, state governors have "police power" during a state of emergency, enabling governors to bypass normal legislative procedures (Tabor, 2022). In Illinois, statutes for emergency power give the governor the ability to restrict freedom of movement, suspend regulatory statutes that might get in the way of emergency responses, and coordinate state resources and state and local police (Tabor). In Illinois, as the governor assumed emergency powers and declared a stay-at-home order, rural areas initially experienced far fewer cases of COVID. This was at play as the Illinois Republican party began its pivot from business conservatism to Trumpism, with Bailey's lawsuit as perhaps the clearest departure point for the party's move toward extremism.

Bailey benefited from the preexisting polarization and resentment between Republicans and Democrats in Illinois. This context provides a dynamic departure point for understanding how even "blue" places are vulnerable to the excesses of right-wing radical populists, especially given our contemporary political structure, constraints on news production embedded journalism norms, and the current structure of the US news industry. Bailey was challenging the rule of law, and in this specific instance, challenging Pritzker's emergency powers as overreach seems reasonable and within bounds – Arguably a very pro-democracy action. As the coverage expanded, Bailey would go on to further justify his lawsuit by trying to distance the pandemic from broader conversations about the Constitution, abuse of powers, and overreach of executive authority. But the language of constitutionalism and liberty – and the democratic process itself – has been used by extremists as a tactic to legitimize antidemocratic politics. Bailey was challenging the rule of law, and in this specific instance, challenging Pritzker's emergency powers as overreach seems reasonable and within bounds – and arguably the most democratic action a politician might take. Certainly, Bailey suing the governor was indeed news – but unfortunately, news norms like objectivity, conflict, and coverage of "knowns" helped push the story along.

Our corpus was almost entirely routine, reported news coverage from mainstream news organizations. Stenographic news coverage in a time of threatened democratic norms is simply not powerful enough to provide a robust check on extremism. For journalists, the use of quotations is a critical way to maintain objectivity and distance. Quoting Bailey directly was the only news value-add, communicating what he actually said to audiences. However, these quotes were rarely enmeshed in supporting analysis that might discredit Bailey's claims about "liberty" and "freedom." When journalists repeated claims by Bailey and others about how their liberty and constitutional rights were threatened, either by Pritzker's emergency order in this case or by another protest to the rule of law, they gave oxygen to these bad faith arguments. By his account, Bailey was not protesting against public health measures but rather against Pritzker violating his constitutional rights. Bailey got to portray himself as a warrior underdog protesting against big government, simply by being quoted in the institutional news media. Even if journalists address the false balance claim and quote actors only in proportion to their relative importance to the story, reiterating Bailey's statements about defending his liberty without pushback or context legitimizes his claims, over and over, in headlines and via continued coverage. There was little coverage about the merits of the lawsuit itself. In fact, the coverage enabled Bailey to so clearly articulate his perspectives such that right-wing news media could simply repurpose AP coverage without any changes.

Regardless of the merit of Bailey's lawsuit, our corpus provides ample evidence of the limitations of mainstream news reporting to adequately contextualize challenges to the rule of law even if conducted through democratic processes. This was just the first of many efforts by Bailey to challenge the rule of law, and it is perhaps particularly clever because the lawsuit appears so immediately justifiable and was conducted within the bounds of the judicial process. As Levitsky and Ziblatt (2018) argue, democracy depends on people willing to accept the outcome of democratic processes (institutional forbearance). Bailey's political activities and statements prior to this lawsuit and in the weeks, months, and years after suggest this challenge was not in good faith. Ironically, antidemocratic politicians often adopt the language of liberty and freedom while seeking to undermine them (Gershberg & Illing, 2022).

Over the course of the next two years, Bailey's authoritarian streak, antidemocratic tendencies, anti-institutionalism, and extreme rural resentment would continue to reveal itself as he accumulated power and influence in the Illinois Republican party. His breakthrough came during the early days of the COVID pandemic, but his extremist politics went far beyond just protesting pandemic restrictions. In the summer of 2020, Bailey complained on his Facebook page that the Republicans' "corn poll" (with popularity shown by corn kernels in jars) at the Illinois state fair was "fake news." On August 5, 2020, he suggested that Pritzker should be jailed. In November 2020, Bailey won his first election to the state Senate seat by 76 percentage points. In February 2021, Bailey announced he would run for governor, and in September 2022, won the Republican state primary. While Bailey was trounced in November 2022 with Pritzker earning 54.9 percent of the vote, throughout his 2022 campaign, Bailey showed his affinity for Republican talking points and conspiracies. In the

October 26, 2022, gubernatorial debate against Pritzker, he said, "Governor Pritzker's family foundation is funding experimental gender surgeries on children across the nation" (Connolly, 2022). His name would make lists of Trump-backed election deniers watched by the national news media. The *New York Times*, in an article headlined, "Darren Bailey, a far-right state senator, will be the Republican nominee for Illinois governor," reported that Bailey was likely helped by Pritzker's advertisements that highlighted his "conservative credentials" (Epstein, 2022).

Bailey was widely credited in the press with spearheading a rightward shift away from establishment Republican politics. *Politico Illinois*' main correspondent's 2022 election analysis appeared in the national edition of *Politico*, noting the state's "big right turn": "A string of victories notched Tuesday night by Donald Trump-backed candidates has realigned the GOP in a place where the party has been pushed out of every statewide office and subjected to Democratic supermajorities in the Legislature" (Kapos, 2022).

In the aftermath of 2022, *Chicago Magazine* spoke with political experts who pointed to the nationalization of local elections away from local issues, "A MAGA Republican in Illinois thinks like a MAGA Republican in Alabama." The article noted how at the primary level, "All up and down the Republican ballot, rural conservatives defeated establishment candidates." In July 2023, Bailey announced his run for US Congress. Democratic redistricting pit Bailey against an incumbent Republican, Rep. Michael Bost. Illinois Rep. Mary Miller, who became infamous for telling an audience in front of the US capitol that "Hitler was right on one thing – "Whoever has the youth has the future. Our children are being propagandised" endorsed Bailey, calling him "MAGA to his core." Bost, however, out-MAGA-ed Bailey, earning Trump's coveted endorsement; given this case study, a candidate to the *right* of Bailey ought to be all the more concerning.

From a political strategy perspective, the current political culture presents an opportunistic moment for a small town politician to gain attention from news media – regional, local, national, or partisan – and promote their politics and persona through the specter of liberty. His rise is both a cautionary tale and a blueprint for other would-be local politicians seeking to capture media attention. The intensity and redundancy of news coverage of the lawsuit, its reach into national, local, and partisan audiences, and the framing of stories around familiar tropes of political journalism gave Bailey a platform for his profile and his politics. The Bailey media storm, then, especially in an age of fragmented politics and hyperpartisan polarization, might well be increasingly understood not as an isolated event but as the start of something pernicious and problematic, especially if the political actor or the jumping-off event is a controversy that seeks to undermine democratic norms.

Scholarly and public complaints about the conflict-driven nature of news, false balance/problematic objectivity, the obsession with known politicians, and beyond are nothing new in media criticism or communication scholarship. Perhaps these flaws were less problematic in a status quo political environment when both major parties at the national, state, and local levels were committed to mostly playing within the bounds of established democratic norms. News coverage was imperfect, but it wasn't providing an unintended runway for extremism. Journalists rely on the same norms, routines, and assessments of newsworthiness to cover other, more alarming threats to democracy, such as threats to free and fair elections and attacks on the independent judiciary. In our current political culture, these enduring problems with news coverage are far more consequential – especially as the Republican party has radicalized.

While we do not expect the institutional news media to function as political opposition to extremist politicians, we do believe that news organizations can more directly advocate for democratic norms. Preliminary research finds that journalists are willing to modify their coverage to more directly center "pro-democracy election frames," wherein journalists focus on the voting and policy positions of candidates rather than reporting on their rhetoric or political strategy (Peterson, McGregor & Block, 2025; Jang & Kreiss, 2024). The Democratic decline in established democracies does not happen overnight, but instead is the slow dureé of gradual acceptance and normalization of attacks on individual liberties, marginalized groups, and support for authoritarian-style leadership.

The American news media and public stakeholders at large need to be aware of the ways media attention can accidentally amplify extremist politicians. Moreover, knowing more about the vulnerabilities of the structure of the news industry itself sheds insight into how this amplification might occur, with homogenous stories repeated across outlets and local, regional, and national news coverage. These concerns are especially important at a time of declining resources for news coverage of state and local politics. The capacity of extremist Republican talking points to hijack political discourse is increasingly concerning because these distortions are fundamentally dangerous to democracy itself – especially those about election denial and a rigged judicial system. The news norms that facilitate democratic life may also facilitate its undoing. While the question of whether the American news media is up to the task of covering extremism, illiberalism, and democratic backsliding is an existential one, the continued inability of mainstream media to cover extremists with a contextual, critical, and pro-democracy framework is a real and present challenge for the future of American democracy.

References

Abernathy, P. M. (2020). *News deserts and ghost newspapers: Will local news survive?* University of North Carolina Press.

Abernathy, P. M. (2022). The state of local news: The 2022 report. *Northwestern University Local News Initiative.* https://localnewsinitiative.northwestern.edu/research/state-of-local-news/2022/report/.

Adams, A. (January 6, 2021). Local reaction to Washington chaos: "Hopefully we can get back to having a decent country." *Effingham Daily News.* https://www.effinghamdailynews.com/news/local_news/local-reaction-to-washington-chaos-hopefully-we-can-get-back-to-having-a-decent-country/article_0f203114-507b-11eb-b1f6-5ba89da456f8.html.

Associated Press (November 5, 2024). AP Race Call: Republican Mike Bost wins reelection to U.S. House in Illinois' 12th Congressional District, AP News. https://apnews.com/article/race-call-bost-wins-illinois-u-s-house-district-db0b3489378842d4a6ee041ab38456ca.

Auxier, B. & Anderson, M. (April 7, 2021). Social media use in 2021. *Pew Research Center.* www.pewresearch.org/internet/2021/04/07/social-media-use-in-2021/.

Ayers-Brown, A. & Petrella, D. (May 3, 2020). "Free exercise of religion" OK'd as order modified; Church had filed federal lawsuit against Pritzker. *Chicago Tribune.*

Bailey, D. [@DarrenBaileyIL]. (December 31, 2023). I'll be here putting together this puzzle waiting for Pritzker to knock on my door and take my guns. [Post]. X. https://x.com/DarrenBaileyIL/status/1741637201161863247.

Barr, J. (January 14, 2022). Joe Kahn is now editing the New York Times. Don't expect a revolution. *The Washington Post.* www.washingtonpost.com/media/2022/06/14/joseph-kahn-new-york-times-twitter-democracy/.

Bartholomé, G., Lecheler, S., & De Vreese, C. (2018). Towards A typology of conflict frames: Substantiveness and interventionism in political conflict news. *Journalism Studies, 19*(12), 1689–1711. https://doi.org/10.1080/1461670X.2017.1299033.

Bellah, R. N. (1967). Civil religion in America. *Daedalus, 96*(1), 1–21. www.jstor.org/stable/20027022.

Bennett, T. M., & Durkin, J. (February 17, 2021). *H.R. 0101, 102nd General Assembly: Urges redoubling conservation.* Illinois House of Representatives.

https://www.ilga.gov/legislation/BillStatus.asp?DocTypeID=HR&DocNum=101&GAID=16&SessionID=110&LegID=131350.

Bennett, W. L., Lawrence, R. G., & Livingston, S. (2008). *When the press fails: Political power and the news media from Iraq to Katrina*. University of Chicago Press.

Bessler, K. (April 3, 2023). Illinois lost more population in 2022. *Advantage News*. https://www.advantagenews.com/news/local/illinois-lost-more-population-in-2022/article_f5056738-cf06-11ed-a29a-ef0d3d69e7fe.html.

Bessler, K. (February 2, 2023). As rural areas lose population, some suggest ways to attract residents. *The Center Square*. www.thecentersquare.com/illinois/article_175440aa-a330-11edba32-c78bceebd3d7.html.

Boydstun, A. E., Hardy, A., & Walgrave, S. (2014). Two faces of media attention: Media storm versus non-storm coverage. *Political Communication, 31*(4), 509–531. https://doi.org/10.1080/10584609.2013.875967.

Burnett, S. (October 28, 2021). Illinois Dems embrace gerrymandering in fight for US House. *Associated Press*. https://apnews.com/article/elections-race-and-ethnicity-philanthropy-barack-obama-state-governments-73d75629c440a971c65e9016476ed869.

Callaghan, T., Moghtaderi, A., Lueck, J., et al. (2021). Correlates and disparities of intention to vaccinate against COVID-19. *Social Science& Medicine, 272*, 113638. https://doi.org/10.1016/j.socscimed.2020.113638.

Callison, C., & Young, M. L. (2019). *Reckoning: Journalism's limits and possibilities*. Oxford University Press.

Carey, J. W. (1974). Journalism and criticism: The case of an undeveloped profession. *The Review of Politics, 36*(2), 227–249.

Carey, J. W. ([1995] 1997). The press, public opinion, and public discourse: On the edge of the postmodern. In *James Carey: A Critical Reader*, edited by E. S. Munson and C. A. Warren, 228257. Minneapolis: University of Minnesota Press.

Carey, M. C. (2017). *The news untold: Community journalism and the failure to confront poverty in Appalachia*. West Virginia University Press.

Carlson, M., Robinson, S., & Lewis, S. C. (2021). *News after Trump: Journalism's crisis of relevance in a changed media culture*. Oxford University Press.

Center for Illinois Politics. (December 6, 2020). *Behind Illinois' blue façade: Growing political polarization*. Center for Illinois Politics. www.centerforillinoispolitics.org/articles/behind-illinois-blue-facade-growing-partisan-polarization.

Chen, Z, Chen, H., Freire, J., Nagler, J. & Tucker, J.A. (2022). What we learned about The Gateway Pundit from its own web traffic data. [Conference presentation]. Workshop proccedings of the 16th International AAAI Conference on Web and Social Media. https://doi.org/10.36190/2022.68.

Collins, E. (2016, Feb. 29). Les Moonves: Trump's run is "damn good for CBS." *Politico*. www.politico.com/blogs/on-media/2016/02/les-moonves-trump-cbs-220001.

Cook, T. E. (2012). *Governing with the news: The news media as a political institution*. University of Chicago Press.

Connolly, D. (October 26, 2022). *Bailey references 'transphobic', 'antisemitic' conspiracy theory at debate. WCIA*. https://www.wcia.com/news/bailey-references-transphobic-antisemitic-conspiracy-theory-at-debate/.

Corley, C. (April 28, 2020). Illinois lawmaker files lawsuit; wants stay-at-home rules lifted. *NPR*. www.npr.org/sections/coronavirus-live-updates/2020/04/28/847620047/illinois-lawmaker-files-lawsuit-wants-stay-at-home-rules-lifted.

Cortes, L. (March 20, 2024). What the Mike Bost, Darren Bailey election results tell us about the Republican party. *Belleville News-Democrat*. https://www.yahoo.com/news/mike-bost-darren-bailey-election-100000551.html.

Cramer, K. J. (2016). *The politics of resentment: Rural consciousness in Wisconsin and the rise of Scott Walker*. University of Chicago Press.

Darr, J. P., Matthew, P. H., & Johanna, L. D. (2021). *Home style opinion: How local newspapers can slow polarization*. Cambridge University Press, 2021.

Deto, R. (January 7, 2021). Block communication family member supports insurrection online as BCI journalists allege management edited stories to downplay the events. *Pittsburgh City Paper*. www.pghcitypaper.com/news/block-communication-family-member-supports-insurrection-onlineas-bci-journalists-allege-management-edited-stories-to-downplay-the-events-18696758.

Diamond, D. (June 2, 2024). In the pandemic, we were told to keep 6 feet apart. There's no science to support that. *Washington Post*. www.washingtonpost.com/health/2024/06/02/six-foot-rule-covid-no-science/.

Dumouchel, D. (2023). Raining on the parties' parade: How media storms disrupt the electoral communicational environment. *Journal of Elections, Public Opinion and Parties, 33*(2), 163–181.

Ellis, D. G. (1999). Research on social interaction and the micro-macro issue. *Research on Language & Social Interaction, 32*(1–2), 31–40.

Elmelund-Præstekær, C., & Wien, C. (2008). What's the fuss about? The interplay of media hypes and politics. *The International Journal of Press/Politics, 13*(3), 247–266.

Entman, R. M. (2004). *Projections of power: Framing news, public opinion, and US foreign policy*. University of Chicago Press.

Epstein, R. J. (2022, June 28). Darren Bailey, a far-right state senator, will be the Republican nominee for Illinois governor. *The New York Times*. https://www.nytimes.com/2022/06/28/us/politics/darren-bailey-illinois-governor-republican.html.

Friedland, L. A., Shah, D. V., Wagner, M. W. et al. (2022). *Battleground: Asymmetric communication ecologies and the erosion of civil society in Wisconsin*. Cambridge University Press.

Gannett Company. (2024). *Gannett fact sheet Q1 2024*. https://www.gannett.com/wp-content/uploads/2024/02/Gannett-Fact-Sheet-Q1-2024.pdf.

Gans, H. J. (1979/2004). *Deciding what's news: A study of CBS evening news, NBC nightly news, Newsweek, and Time*. Northwestern University Press.

Gershberg, Z. & Illing, S. (2022). *The paradox of democracy: Free speech, open media, and perilous persuasion*. University of Chicago Press.

Gruszczynski, M. (2020). How media storms and topic diversity influence agenda fragmentation. *International Journal of Communication*, *14*, 22.

Harcup, T., & O'Neill, D. (2017). What is news? News values revisited (again). *Journalism Studies*, *18*(12), 1470–1488.

Hardy, A. (2017). The mechanisms of media storms. In *From media hype to Twitter storm*, edited by P. Vasterman, 133–148. Amsterdam University Press.

Hassell, H. J., Holbein, J. B., & Miles, M. R. (2020). There is no liberal media bias in which news stories political journalists choose to cover. *Science Advances*, 6(14), eaay9344.

Hayes, D., & Lawless, J. L. (2021). *News hole: The demise of local journalism and political engagement*. Cambridge University Press.

Herbst, S. (1998). *Reading public opinion: How political actors view the democratic process*. University of Chicago Press.

Hester, J. B., & Gibson, R. (2007). The agenda-setting function of national versus local media: A time-series analysis for the issue of same-sex marriage. *Mass Communication & Society*, *10*(3), 299–317.

Hopkins, D. J. (2018). *The increasingly United States: How and why American political behavior nationalized*. University of Chicago Press.

Illinois Governor Pritzker Announces Stay-at-Home Order. (March 21, 2020) *The National Law Review*.

Illinois Local Journalism Task Force (January 2024). An assessment of the news crisis and policy options. https://dceo.illinois.gov/content/dam/soi/en/web/dceo/events/local-journalism-task-force/local-journalism-task-force-final-report-january-2024.pdf.

Illinois Press Association (n.d.). IPA media kit. www.illinoispress.org/Advertising/IPAMediaKit.aspx.

References

Illinois' Stay-at-Home Order Extended Through April, Pritzker Announces. (March 31, 2020). NBC Chicago. www.nbcchicago.com/news/local/illinois-stay-at-home-order-expected-to-be-extended-sources/2247274/.

Jaffe, L. (October 20, 2017). *Defining downstate illinois*. ProPublica. www.propublica.org/article/defining-downstate-illinois.

Jaidka, K., Fischer, S., Lelkes, Y., & Wang, Y. (2023). News nationalization in a digital age: An examination of how local protests are covered and curated online. *The ANNALS of the American Academy of Political and Social Science, 707*(1), 189–207.

Jang, H., & Kreiss, D. (2024). Safeguarding the peaceful transfer of power: Pro-democracy electoral frames and journalist coverage of election deniers during the 2022 US midterm elections. *The International Journal of Press/Politics*, 19401612241235819.

Kapos, S. (June 29, 2022). Illinois GOP takes big right turn with primary victories. *Politico*. www.politico.com/news/2022/06/29/illinois-gop-takes-big-right-turn-with-primary-victories.

Kapos, S. (2023). Illinois Republican Darren Bailey challenges Rep. Mike Bost, *Politico*. www.politico.com/news/2023/07/04/illinois-darren-bailey-mike-bost-00104658.

Karlsson, M., Ferrer Conill, R., & Örnebring, H. (2023). Recoding journalism: Establishing normative dimensions for a twenty-first century news media. *Journalism Studies, 24*(5), 1–20.

Karppinen, K., Moe, H., & Svensson, J. (2008). Habermas, Mouffe and political communication: A case for theoretical eclecticism. *Javnost-the Public, 15*(3), 5–21.

Katz, A. J. (April 29, 2020). April 2020 cable news show ranker: Bret Baier, Martha MacCallum, Tucker Carlson, Chris Cuomo among top-rated hosts of the month. *Adweek*. https://www.adweek.com/tvnewser/april-2020-cable-news-show-ranker-bret-baier-martha-maccallum-tucker-carlson-chris-cuomo-among-top-rated-hosts-of-the-month/.

Kovach, B., & Rosenstiel, T. (2021). *The elements of journalism, revised and updated What newspeople should know and the public should expect*. Crown.

Jang, H., & Kreiss, D. (2024). Safeguarding the peaceful transfer of power: Pro-democracy electoral frames and journalist coverage of election deniers during the 2022 US midterm elections. *The International Journal of Press/Politics*, 19401612241235819.

Landis, K. (January 7, 2021). Miller votes against certifying Biden as president. *Effingham Daily News*.

Levendusky, M. S. (2022). How does local TV news change viewers' attitudes? The case of Sinclair broadcasting. *Political Communication, 39*(1), 23–38.

Levitsky, S., & Ziblatt, D. (2018). *How democracies die.* Crown.

Markham, A. N., Harris, A., & Luka, M. E. (2021). Massive and microscopic sensemaking during COVID-19 times. *Qualitative Inquiry, 27*(7), 759–766.

Marwick, A., & Lewis, R. (2017). *Media manipulation and disinformation online.* Data & Society Research Institute.

Mason, L. (2018). *Uncivil agreement: How politics became our identity.* University of Chicago Press.

McKinney, D. (January 10, 2022). Illinois is thought to be a blue state. So why is the so much of the state so red? *St. Louis Public Radio.* www.stlpr.org/government-politics-issues/2022-01-10/illinois-is-thought-to-be-a-blue-state-so-why-is-so-much-of-the-state-so-red.

McKinney, D. (September 22, 2022). Examining the record: Darren Bailey pushed to fix the state's ills, but critics call him ineffective. *WSIU.* www.wsiu.org/state-of-illinois/2022-09-30/examining-the-record-darren-bailey-pushed-to-fix-the-states-ills-but-critics-call-him-ineffective.

Mediaite. (April 29, 2020). Daily ratings. www.mediaite.com/category/daily-ratings/.

Meisel, H. (October 6, 2022). Pritzker, Bailey square off in first of two debates, each accusing the other of lying. *NPR Illinois.* www.nprillinois.org/government-politics/2022-10-06/pritzker-bailey-square-off-in-first-of-two-debates-each-accusing-the-other-of-lying.

Mervoush, S., Miller, C. C., & Paris, F. (March 18, 2024). What the data says about pandemic school closures, four years later. *New York Times The Upshot.* www.nytimes.com/2024/03/18/upshot/pandemic-school-closures-data.html.

Metzger, Z. (October 23, 2024). The state of local news: The 2024 report. *Northwestern University Local News Initiative.* https://localnewsinitiative.northwestern.edu/projects/state-of-local-news/2024/report/.

Nah, S., Kwon, H. K., Liu, W., and McNealy, J. E. (2021). Communication infrastructure, social media, and civic participation across geographically diverse communities in the United States. *Communication Studies, 72*(3), 437–455.

Nielsen, R. K. (Ed.). (2015). *Local journalism: The decline of newspapers and the rise of digital media.* Bloomsbury.

Örnebring, H., & Karlsson, M. (2022). *Journalistic autonomy: The genealogy of a concept.* University of Missouri Press.

Padgett, J., Dunaway, J. L., & Darr, J. P. (2019). As seen on TV? How gatekeeping makes the US house seem more extreme. *Journal of Communication, 69*(6), 696–719.

Paul Simon Policy Institute. (2007). *Party competition in illinois: Republican prospects in a blue state.*

Pearson, R. & Gorner, J. (March 03, 2024,). Downstate race highlights GOP move to right: Trump looms large as Bailey challenges Bost for Congress. *Chicago Tribune.* https://digitaledition.chicagotribune.com/tribune/article_popover.aspx?guid=a2889758-a24e-4ff0-8678-1c89faf0cf90.

Peterson, E. (2021). Paper cuts: How reporting resources affect political news coverage. *American Journal of Political Science, 65*(2), 443–459.

Peterson, E., & Dunaway, J. (2023). The new news barons: Investment ownership reduces newspaper reporting capacity. *The ANNALS of the American Academy of Political and Social Science, 707*(1), 74–89.

Peterson, E., McGregor, S. C., & Block, R. (2025). Election denial as a news coverage dilemma: A survey experiment with local journalists. *Political Communication*, 1–20.

Pew Research Center. (2023). *News platform fact sheet.* Pew Research Center. www.pewresearch.org/journalism/fact-sheet/news-platform-fact-sheet/.

Pickard, V. (2019). *Democracy without journalism?: Confronting the misinformation society.* Oxford University Press.

Pritzker, J. B. Executive Order 2020-10. (March 20, 2020). www.illinois.gov/government/executive-orders/executive-order.executive-order-number-10.2020.html.

Pritzker, J. B. Executive Order 2020-32. (April 30, 2020). www.illinois.gov/government/executive-orders/executive-order.executive-order-number-32.2020.html.

Pritzker breaks down changes coming to Illinois' stay-at-home order. (April 30, 2020). *NBC Chicago.* www.nbcchicago.com/news/coronavirus/pritzker-breaks-down-changes-coming-to-illinois-stay-at-home-order/2264577/.

The Righting. (n.d.). Election year audience erosion continues for right-wing websites. https://therighting.com/traffic-reports/election-year-audience-erosion-continues-for-right-wing-websites/.

Rosen, J. (1999). *What are journalists for?* Yale University Press.

Schmidt, H. (April 4, 2022). *4 of 10 of the last Illinois governors went to prison.* Illinois Policy. www.illinoispolicy.org/4-of-illinois-past-10-governors-went-to-prison/.

Searles, K., & Banda, K. K. (2019). But her emails! How journalistic preferences shaped election coverage in 2016. *Journalism, 20*(8), 1052–1069.

Simpson, D. Rossi, M. R., & Gradel, T. (2021). *Corruption spikes in Illinois: Anti-corruption report #13*. University of Illinois Chicago. https://pols.uic.edu/wp-content/uploads/sites/273/2021/02/Corruption-Spikes-in-IL-Anti-Corruption-Rpt-13-final2.-1.pdf.

Smith, M. (March 2, 2022). Powerful ex-Illinois house speaker is indicted on federal charges. *The New York Times*. www.nytimes.com/2022/03/02/us/michael-madigan-illinois-indictment.html.

Tabor, J. (January 6, 2022). Illinois has been subject to Pritzker's emergency powers for nearly 22 months. Where does this power come from? *Illinois Policy*. https://www.illinoispolicy.org/illinois-has-been-subject-to-pritzkers-emergency-powers-for-nearly-22-months-where-does-this-power-come-from/.

Tuchman, G. (1972). Objectivity as strategic ritual: An examination of newsmen's notions of objectivity. *American Journal of Sociology*, 77(4), 660–679.

USDA. (2013). Rural-Urban Continuum Code. www.ers.usda.gov/data-products/rural-urban-continuum-codes/.

Usher, N. (2014). *Making news at the New York Times*. University of Michigan Press.

Usher, N. (2016). The constancy of immediacy: From printing press to digital age. In *The crisis of journalism reconsidered: Democratic culture, professional codes, digital future*, edited by J. C. Alexander, E. B. Breese, and M. Luengo, 170–189. Cambridge University Press.

Usher, N. (2018). Breaking news production processes in US metropolitan newspapers: Immediacy and journalistic authority. *Journalism*, 19(1), 21–36.

Usher, N. (2019). Journalism's biggest challenge? Journalists. *Journalism*, 20(1), 140–143.

Usher, N. (2021). *News for the rich, white, and blue: How place and power distort American journalism*. Columbia University Press.

Usher, N. (2022). *Fighting COVID-19 in Illinois: A case study of local health department officials' reliance on Facebook*. Open Markets Institute. www.openmarketsinstitute.org/publications/fighting-covid-19-in-illinois-a-case-study-of-local-health-department-officials-reliance-on-facebook.

Usher, N. (2023). Delegitimizing rural public health departments: How decaying local news ecologies, misinformation, and radicalization undermine community storytelling networks. *The ANNALS of the American Academy of Political and Social Science*, 707(1), 90–108.

Usher, N., & Kim-Leffingwell, S. (2023). How loud does the watchdog bark? A reconsideration of losing local journalism, news nonprofits, and political corruption. *The International Journal of Press/Politics*, 19401612231186939.

Usher, N., Wong, A. T., Raynal, I. R., Bigman-Galimore, C., & Maslowska, E. (2023). Localizing COVID-19 public health department outreach on digital platforms: The role of discoverability, reach, and moderation for illinois' COVID-19 vaccination rates. *American Behavioral Scientist, 30*, 0002764 2231166884.

Vasterman, P. (2005). Media-hype: Self-reinforcing news waves, journalistic standards and the construction of social problems. *European Journal of Communication, 20*(4), 508–530.

Vorva, J. (July 29, 2020). *Lions, Kiwanis and Rotary clubs struggle to recruit new, younger members. Chicago Tribune.*

Wagner, M. W., & Gruszczynski, M. (2018). Who gets covered? Ideological extremity and news coverage of members of the US Congress, 1993 to 2013. *Journalism & Mass Communication Quarterly, 95*(3), 670–690.

Walgrave, S., Boydstun, A. E., Vliegenthart, R., & Hardy, A. (2017). The nonlinear effect of information on political attention: media storms and US congressional hearings. *Political Communication, 34*(4), 548–570.

Watts, M. D., Domke, D., Shah, D. V., & Fan, D. P. (1999). Elite cues and media bias in presidential campaigns: Explaining public perceptions of a liberal press. *Communication Research, 26*(2), 144–175.

Weber, M., Peter A., & Napoli, P. M. 2019. Local news on Facebook: Assessing the critical information needs served through Facebook's TodayIn feature. Durham, NC: Duke University Sanford School of Public Policy. https://hsjmc.umn.edu/sites/hsjmc.umn.edu/files/2019-9/Facebook%20Critical%20Information%20Needs%20Report.pdf.

Wells, C., Friedland, L. A., Hughes, C. et al. (2021). News media use, talk networks, and anti-elitism across geographic location: Evidence from Wisconsin. *The International Journal of Press/Politics, 26*(2), 438–463.

Wenzel, A. (Ed.) (2023). "Pink Slime": Partisan journalism and the future of local news. Tow Center for Digital Journalism. Columbia University. https://towcenter.columbia.edu/content/publications-0#!#views-display-5.

Wippell, J. G. R. (2024). "To protect and serve"... and rule: constitutional sheriffs and the emergence of far-right extremism within local politics. *Politics, Groups, and Identities*, 1–20. https://doi.org/10.1080/21565503.2024.2430524.

Wolfsfeld, G. (2013). The politics-media-politics principle: Towards a more comprehensive approach to political communication. Paper, American Political Science Association 2013 Annual Meeting.

Wolfsfeld, G., Segev, E., & Sheafer, T., 2013. Social media and the Arab Spring: Politics comes first. *The International Journal of Press/Politics, 18*(2), 115–137.

Wolfsfeld, G., Sheafer, T., & Althaus, S. (2022). *Building theory in political communication: The politics-media politics approach.* Oxford University Press.

Zeilinger, E. L., Brunevskaya, N., Wurzer, J. et al. (2024). Effectiveness of cloth face masks to prevent viral spread: A meta-analysis. *Journal of Public Health*, *46*(1), e84–e90. https://doi.org/10.1093/pubmed/fdad205.

Acknowledgments

We would like to extend our gratitude to the two undergraduate research assistants at the University of San Diego, Abigale Baines and Mia Delmonico

Cambridge Elements

Politics and Communication

Stuart Soroka
University of California

Stuart Soroka is a Professor in the Department of Communication at the University of California, Los Angeles, and Adjunct Research Professor at the Center for Political Studies at the Institute for Social Research, University of Michigan. His research focuses on political communication, political psychology, and the relationships between public policy, public opinion, and mass media. His books with Cambridge University Press include The Increasing Viability of Good News (2021, with Yanna Krupnikov), Negativity in Democratic Politics (2014), Information and Democracy (forthcoming, with Christopher Wlezien) and Degrees of Democracy (2010, with Christopher Wlezien).

About the Series

Cambridge Elements in Politics and Communication publishes research focused on the intersection of media, technology, and politics. The series emphasizes forward-looking reviews of the field, path-breaking theoretical and methodological innovations, and the timely application of social-scientific theory and methods to current developments in politics and communication around the world.

Cambridge Elements

Politics and Communication

Elements in the Series

Power in Ideas: A Case-Based Argument for Taking Ideas Seriously in Political Communication
Kirsten Adams and Daniel Kreiss

Economic News: Antecedents and Effects
Rens Vliegenthart, Alyt Damstra, Mark Boukes and Jeroen Jonkman

The Increasing Viability of Good News
Stuart Soroka and Yanna Krupnikov

Digital Transformations of the Public Arena
Andreas Jungherr and Ralph Schroeder

Battleground: Asymmetric Communication Ecologies and the Erosion of Civil Society in Wisconsin
Lewis A. Friedland, Dhavan V. Shah, Michael W. Wagner, Katherine J. Cramer, Chris Wells and Jon Pevehouse

Constructing Political Expertise in the News
Kathleen Searles, Yanna Krupnikov, John Barry Ryan and Hillary Style

The YouTube Apparatus
Kevin Munger

How News Coverage of Misinformation Shapes Perceptions and Trust
Emily Thorson

Angry and Wrong: The Emotional Dynamics of Partisan Media and Political Misperceptions
Brian E. Weeks

Social Media Democracy Mirage: How Social Media News Fuels a Politically Uninformed Participatory Democracy
Homero Gil de Zúñiga, Hugo Marcos-Marne, Manuel Goyanes and Rebecca Scheffauer

Political Representation as Communicative Practice
Fabio Wolkenstein and Christopher Wratil

Amplifying Extremism: Small Town Politicians, Media Storms, and American Journalism
Nik Usher and Jessica C. Hagman

A full series listing is available at: www.cambridge.org/EPCM

For EU product safety concerns, contact us at Calle de José Abascal, 56–1°, 28003 Madrid, Spain or eugpsr@cambridge.org.

www.ingramcontent.com/pod-product-compliance
Ingram Content Group UK Ltd.
Pitfield, Milton Keynes, MK11 3LW, UK
UKHW021459220625
459949UK00018B/490